Cowgirl Chef

TEXAS COOKING

with

A FRENCH ACCENT

by ELLISE PIERCE

RUNNING PRESS
PHILADELPHIA · LONDON

Published by Running Press,
A Member of the Perseus Books Group

Books published by Running Press are available at special discounts for bulk purchases
in the United States by corporations, institutions, and other organizations. For more
information, please contact the Special Markets Department at the Perseus Books
Group, 2300 Chestnut Street, Suite 200, Philadelphia, PA 19103, or call (800) 810-
4145, ext. 5000, or e-mail special.markets@perseusbooks.com.

ISBN 978-0-7624-4463-2
Library of Congress Control Number: 2011944642

E-book ISBN 978-0-7624-4505-9

9 8 7 6 5 4 3 2 1
Digit on the right indicates the number of this printing

Book design by Amanda Richmond
Edited by Jennifer Kasius
Typography: Clarendon, ITC Clearface, and Samantha

Running Press Book Publishers
2300 Chestnut Street
Philadelphia, PA 19103-4371

Visit us on the web!
www.runningpress.com

Some recipes in this book call for the use of raw eggs.
Please note that the consumption of raw or undercooked eggs may
increase the risk of food-borne illness, and is especially not advised
for young children, pregnant women, and the elderly.

to Mom

Contents

How I Found My Inner Cowgirl Chef ...7

Cowgirl Chef Kitchen Basics ...14

CowgirlSpeak: A Trail Guide ...18

CHAPTER 1
Appetizers: Old Favorites and New Beginnings ...23

CHAPTER 2
Cowgirlified Frenchy ...57

CHAPTER 3
Souped Up ...83

CHAPTER 4
Greens ...117

CHAPTER 5
Tacos, Tarts, and Tartines ...153

CHAPTER 6
Riding Side-Saddle: Veggies ...199

CHAPTER 7
From the Farm and Sea ...235

CHAPTER 8
Desserts ...275

CHAPTER 9
Tex-Mex 101 ...311

Epilogue ...325

Acknowledgments ...326

Index ...328

HOW I FOUND MY INNER
COWGIRL CHEF

After a year in Paris, I was ready to call it quits.

I had completely given up. Given up on the relationship I had moved halfway across the world for. Given up on learning the language. Given up on myself.

My freelance writing career was all but over. Magazines that I'd written for had merged with others, stopped using outside contributors, or simply gone under. The future of journalism looked bleak, and mine looked worse. I had less than 100 euros in my bank account, and my credit card was maxed out. I needed to do something … and quick.

I wanted to move back to Texas, but couldn't afford the plane ticket.

Home was horse country, a college town called Denton, about a half-hour north of Dallas and Fort Worth, where I learned to ride bareback, fearlessly and at full gallop, after school.

Back then, Denton was still a small town, with its old-fashioned square and turn-of-the-century courthouse. It had one high school, two movie theaters (plus a drive-in on the north side of town), a hamburger joint called Johnny's, a Sonic, and Luby's cafeteria, where we'd sometimes go for chicken-fried steak.

I always felt like Denton lived in the shadow of the two bigger, more interesting cities to the south: Dallas, with its flashy glass buildings and air of sophistication, and Fort Worth, with its deep western roots and frontier confidence. I wanted to be like both of those places. I wanted to get out of Denton. I wanted something more.

Early on, I learned that I could explore a world beyond my own through food. Traveling to go out to eat was something that my family did on a fairly regular basis—Dallas for Greek or Italian, Fort Worth for Chinese or Tex-Mex—and closer to home, in elementary school, when other kids were playing kickball, I'd hop on my bike to go to Dairy Queen for a Buster Bar, or to Leroy's Drive-In Grocery for a chopped beef barbecue sandwich. It was my early recognition of eating as adventure.

I saw cooking as its own adventure, too. By junior high, when I was baking batches of chocolate chip or oatmeal cookies, or making my own fudge, I'd lose myself in the process of it all, captivated by the magic that happens along the way when this becomes that with a little heat from the stove or the oven.

When I wasn't cooking, my mom was. I'd sit on a stool and watch while she spun her beaters around a big Tupperware bowl in clockwise and counter-clockwise motion, thumping them against the sides. We usually had homemade cakes for dessert after dinner, and the table was always set the same as it would be if we were having company: the forks, knives, and spoons, lined up and in their proper places. Bread always had a basket, and its own plate. Food was passed from the left to the right. It didn't matter whether we were having Beef Stroganoff or black-eyed peas and cornbread, it was always like this. I never knew any other way.

Dinnertime was an event, and the food, no matter how simple, was always the star.

By the time I was twelve, I had a subscription to *Gourmet*.

In the spring of 2005, through the same friends who had introduced us 10 years before, Xavier (the Frenchman known hereafter as "X") and I finally hit it off. We drove to a friend's wedding in Muskogee, Oklahoma, singing to the Isley Brothers in the car with the windows rolled down. We drank Champagne and giggled and laughed all weekend. We danced all night.

When he left to go back to Paris, I thought he was the one.

For the next two years, we flew back and forth to see each other every couple of months, for a week or two at a time. Each visit unfolded like the pages of a clichéd romance novel, with gifts of French chocolates and lingering dinners over wine in tiny French bistros, followed by walks along the Seine, and a stop on the Pont des Arts (a.k.a. "the Lovers Bridge") for a kiss. Then came the goodbyes, a blur of jetlag and heartache, the time apart, the missed phone calls. The seven-hour time difference was difficult, the stretches of time between visits unbearable.

Finally I ran out of frequent-flier miles. We both decided that one of us had to move … or we needed to break up.

X had a full-time job. I was a freelance writer. I could work from anywhere, I figured. Why not from Paris?

So I rented out my house, packed up my cowboy boots and Cuisinarts big and small, and called the movers.

February is the coldest month of the year in Paris. At least it was when I arrived in 2007.

But if it was bitter outside, it was warm in our new apartment. X and I picked out paint for the walls, and bought rugs and furniture to make things cozy. We settled in.

Sort of. Feeling at home in a foreign country has a lot less to do with unpacking books and cookware, and a lot more to do with speaking the language; and on that front, I was failing miserably. My French was a mishmash of words that I remembered from college and high school, which was useless because I couldn't string them together in a way that made any sense. At the local boulangerie I'd be harshly corrected by the old woman behind the counter—she pretended she didn't understand and made me repeat myself two, sometimes, three times. It was humiliating. I stopped buying bread there.

As much as I struggled with the language, and knew that I needed to spend more time studying French, I felt even more pressure to find work. Months went by without any income, something that had never happened to me before.

I soon grew tired of the cold and the rain, of not being understood. I was homesick for my friends, my family, and the big sunny skies of Texas. X didn't understand why I wasn't happy. We were together in Paris. Wasn't that what I wanted? Wasn't that enough?

Actually, no. Turns out, we didn't know each other at all. I was lost with him and without him.

So I retreated to the only world I knew: the kitchen. In the midst of chaos and the unknown, the kitchen was safe, predictable. Among the teaspoons and cups and well-sharpened knives, I found order. Things made sense. It felt like home.

I couldn't order a loaf of bread in perfect French, but I could bake one. So I started exploring and discovering. I learned that French flour isn't anything like what we have back home—it's milled and mixed to standards I still have trouble getting my head around. The butter has a higher fat content. The crème fraîche a richer, heavier version of sour cream. It took awhile, and many disasters, to understand the differences between American and French ingredients, but I'd been in the kitchen all my life. I knew that if I kept trying, I could make my recipes work.

It took some improvising. When I ran out of salsa and flour tortillas, Tex-Mex staples that I'd bring back to Paris from home, I started making my own. I didn't have a *comal*, so X bought me a cast-iron *crêpière* to use instead. I went to the weekly markets and found sweet potatoes, or black-eyed peas, and yellow squash, ingredients that were familiar.

The more I cooked, the less homesick I felt.

But after a while, there was only so much that a batch of cookies could do to lift my spirits.

I needed work. But I didn't know what I could do in France. Then I met a couple of American women who'd invited me to be part of their small expat support group, which got together every few weeks to help one another brainstorm about new careers. Turns out, my predicament wasn't that unusual. Most of us move here with a dream, sometimes just the dream of living in Paris. Then the money runs out. Reality sets in. So it wasn't just me: we were all trying to figure out how to make a buck. Or a euro. Anything.

I thought about teaching yoga, like I'd done in Dallas a few years earlier, and it seemed to everyone like a good enough idea … until I took guacamole, salsa, and some chicken empanadas to a meeting. "Yoga!" one of the women said, waving her empanada in the air. "Why aren't you cooking? Catering to other homesick expats?"

Cooking? In the culinary capital of the world? Sure, I'd always thrown dinner parties, but I was a writer. It was one of the more farfetched things I'd heard … but I was out of ideas.

So I spent the next two months building a website, and by September of that year, Cowgirl Tacos, a Tex-Mex catering company, was born. I gave myself a month to see if it would work, just one month, and if it didn't, then I was going to borrow the money to move back to Texas.

A funny thing happened after my website went live. I met a woman who worked with the State Department—she asked if I'd ever thought about offering cooking classes, because, she said, if I did, she'd get a group together to take them.

For the next four weeks, Melinda, Julie, Debbie, and Valorie sat around my kitchen table every Wednesday night, and drank margaritas while I taught them the differences between jalapeños and habaneros, and explained the importance of corn in Mexican cuisine. We rolled out flour tortillas, pressed corn tortillas, and made enchiladas. We made guacamole and salsa, too. But more than that, over those few weeks, friendships were hatched that remain today, even though Melinda's now in Beijing, Julie's in Angola, and Valorie has moved on to Madrid.

After the fourth class, and we'd all hugged and they walked out my door, I was so happy, feeling like those classes were the most rewarding thing that I'd ever done, and the most fun, ever—but I was also terribly sad, because now it was over.

Which of course, it wasn't. It was only the beginning.

When I announced a new series of classes that next week, they filled up in a day.

So I started writing a blog, and called it Cowgirl Chef, to promote the cooking classes and catering business, which was providing new and steady income, something that freelance hadn't done in years. Suddenly I was too busy to leave Paris.

And I was happy for the first time in years. I had a focus. I had friends. I was doing something that I loved, and was actually making money sharing a passion I'd had all my life.

I started seeing Paris differently, with a new curiosity. I'd go to the grocery store and to the markets and notice all sorts of things that I hadn't seen before. I once counted thirty-nine (!) different types of sponges at the Casino. I'd wander down the cereal aisle and see if I could find one box without chocolate (nearly impossible). I tried new recipes — French, not American. I bought a madeleine pan. I ate yogurt, plain, with a swirl of honey, just like X did. I made crêpes.

I found inspiration all around me. In the restaurants that X and I would go to. In the weekly markets. In French cooking magazines. My life was opening up.

I kept teaching classes and catering and soon, besides my own Cowgirl Chef blog, I was writing a Cowgirl Chef column for publications back in the States. I was developing dozens of recipes each month. I began making videos, too.

I also began to cook differently. Whereas I'd started cooking recipes from home to ease my homesickness, I soon found that I was ready to try something new. Something French. I bought pans in all shapes and sizes, and made tarts both savory and sweet. I bought a fire gun to perfect the *crème brûlée.* When my baby Cuisinart broke, I bought a new one, a French one. I stopped thinking about moving home altogether. There was too much to experience, to taste, and to make, right here.

One week, I'd experiment with vinaigrettes; another, I'd work on meringues, or puff pastry, or soufflés. I bought vegetables I'd never seen in my life—the pre-Roman, celery-looking, artichoke-tasting *cardons* (cardoons) and cooked them up in a tart, with a recipe that I made up on the spot. I became hooked on the tiny French pumpkin, *potimarron,* and made soups, tarts, and ice cream with it. I fell in love with the knobby pink *topinambours* (Jerusalem artichokes), which I roasted and tossed with cauliflower or puréed into soups. I cooked with a new sense of adventure, and with the confidence that if it didn't work out, I'd just do it again. I became fearless once more... this time in my French kitchen.

I was cooking all the time. And I was having the time of my life.

But when someone suggested I write a cookbook, I thought, *Seriously? Me?*

Then it hit me that besides cooking for people and teaching them what I knew about food, I'd been writing and testing new recipes, which was what I loved most. When I wasn't in the kitchen, I was thinking about food, talking about food, or reading about food. Maybe, just maybe, I could do it.

My inner chef had finally caught up with my outer cowgirl. My Le Creuset-crammed kitchen was on par with my boots-filled closet. Cowgirl Chef, I realized, is who I'd always been. I just had to move to Paris to find her.

COWGIRL CHEF
KITCHEN BASICS

Even though I love to cook, I don't love spending an entire day in the kitchen any more than anyone else does. So I've outfitted myself with a few tools to help me do what I need to do faster and more efficiently. These are the tools that help me get the job done each day.

MACHINES

I've had the same heavy-duty white **KitchenAid stand mixer** for almost twenty-five years. It's made hundreds of batches of cookies and cakes, whipped more egg whites for soufflés and mousses than I can count, kneaded bread, and even ground meat. If you have only one appliance in your kitchen, let this be it.

I've got both **a large and a small food processor**, and I use them both all the time. The small one's great for making pestos, mayonnaises, and vinaigrettes. And it'll chop a big batch of garlic into a nice small mince that you can keep in a jar with some olive oil in the fridge for a few days; I do this when I've got a week's worth of cooking ahead of me and want to save time (you can do the same thing with onions and shallots). The large food processor is my go-to helper for pie and tart crusts; shredded cabbage and carrots, and small batches of bread doughs, like corn and flour tortillas.

I use my **heavy-duty blender** every single day. Mine's made of sturdy thick glass, not plastic. It's great for post-yoga smoothies, perfectly creamy soups, salsas and sauces, and puréed chiles and super-concentrated *moles*.

A **hand (or immersion) blender** is great for blending things that don't need to be too finely puréed, like some soups, and salsas, potatoes, and other veggies.

MEASURING STUFF

Invest in a good **kitchen timer**, and use it. It'll prevent overcooked cakes and cookies, and keep your kitchen running smoothly.

Buy two **oven thermostats**, and put them in different parts of your oven so you'll know where the hottest spots are. That way, as you bake, you can make adjustments, and turn your cookies around so one side isn't twice as brown as the other.

A **candy thermometer** will help you make perfect caramels—and fried chicken, too. You can't make either without one of these.

To be on the safe side, I always use a **meat thermometer** for chicken, and other meats that need to be cooked to a certain temperature, such as pork.

I know you don't want to hear this, but a **kitchen scale** will keep your measurements exact. That's what we use in France (as does most of the rest of the world) and it's a lot easier than cups once you get the hang of it.

The next time you're wandering down the school-supplies aisle, pick up a **wooden ruler**, just like the one that you used to have in your yellow school box. My mom told me about this: It's a great tool for measuring the depth and width of pans, etc. I keep my kitchen ruler in a drawer next to the stove, and use it all the time.

SHARP STUFF

Everyone needs a **zester**, not just for lemons, limes, and oranges, but for finely grating hard cheeses, too. It's an inexpensive and indispensable tool you'll use constantly.

I have a drawerful of knives, but I only really use three—my **7- inch santoku**, a **paring knife** and a **small serrated knife**. I also have a **long serrated knife**, for cutting bread.

I rely on **kitchen scissors** for tons of things—to cut slices of pizza, flat tarts and croustades, and to snip herbs from my garden.

Chicken shears are crazy-looking, super-sharp snippers, but they're exactly what you need to cut up your own chickens. You'll save tons of money by doing it this way.

I found a **serrated vegetable peeler** in Paris and it changed my life. Made for tomatoes, it'll peel anything with tricky, hard-to-remove skin, from peaches to butternut squash.

HANDS-ON STUFF

I have lots of **wooden spoons, tongs** (which do double-duty as lemon and lime squeezers), **silicone brushes, heatproof spatulas** and **whisks** of all sizes. When I want a strong shot of garlic, I use my **garlic press**—it's a heck of a lot easier than peeling cloves.

STUFF THAT ADDS LOTS OF FLAVOR

I make a lot of vinaigrettes, pestos, flavored oils, and salsas, because they're fast and easy. The key is having lots of **fresh herbs** on hand, whether you're growing your own (the best and most cost-efficient way) or buying them at the market. I can't say enough about fresh herbs or the difference using them will make in your cooking. They can liven up the dullest of things —even those mashed potatoes in the fridge from yesterday.

I use oils and vinegars, together and on their own, to flavor everything from salads, fruits, and veggies, to all sorts of meats and fish. As a general rule, I use olive oil and grapeseed oil interchangeably for my vinaigrettes, but also use nut oils. Walnut, hazelnut, and pistachio oils are some of my favorites; they're a bit pricey, but you don't need a lot to make a big impact. I've always got sherry vinegar, Champagne vinegar, red wine vinegar, balsamic vinegar, and apple cider vinegar on hand, too.

And let's not overlook **sea salt** and **freshly ground black pepper**. Sea salt because it tastes brighter and cleaner than table salt, and has a higher mineral content. Never white pepper. Please.

COWGIRLSPEAK:
A TRAIL GUIDE

FLOUR, SUGAR, EGGS,
MILK, AND BUTTER: THE LOWDOWN

We have lots of different flours in France, but in this book, whenever flour is mentioned, unless otherwise noted, I'm referring to all-purpose flour. All eggs should be large, all milk whole. Butter's unsalted. When I refer to cream, I mean whipping cream. If I'm talking about crème fraîche or sour cream, I'll be sure to spell it out clearly. I use powdered sugar, and call it that, because I think confectioners' sugar sounds silly. (Have you ever said I need a box of confectioners' sugar? Have you ever put that on your grocery list? Of course you haven't.) Unless you live in France, in which case it's *sucre glace*, or icing sugar, which is what it's also called in the U.K.

WHEN SIZE DOESN'T MATTER

I know lots of cookbooks are nitpicky about this, and will often tell you if you should use a small onion or a medium carrot, or whatever. I don't do much size prescribing for a couple of reasons: One, my large onion might be your medium; and two, it often really doesn't matter that much, so I try not to micromanage when it's not necessary. On the other hand, when it does matter, when size does count, I'll let you know.

COOKING TIMES AND
OVEN TEMPERATURES

The more you cook, the more you rely on your eyes and nose, and the less you depend on the clock. I've got two thermostats in my oven to let me know when the temperature is going up or down, but my oven's a bit crazy, and as much as I try to manage things, in the end, I trust what I see, smell, and touch, to tell me when something's ready. Same goes for the stovetop. I've made suggestions about temperature and flame and cook times, and I've given visual cues about doneness whenever possible. Interpret my recipes using your own good judgment and simply adjust as you go. That's the Cowgirl way.

SWAP IT, DOUBLE-DUTY, AND COWGIRL TIPS

I've become the queen of the swap-out. If I don't have cheddar, I'll use Comté; if I'm fresh out of crème fraîche, I'll use yogurt. I didn't used to be so thrifty and flexible, but in Paris, when the stores are closed, they're closed, and a girl's gotta eat. But resourcefulness is a great thing to cultivate even if you've got a 24-hour grocery store down the street—it makes good sense not to waste, and it makes cooking even more fun when you know the rules can be bent a little (and in some cases, a whole lot). I've guided you to possible substitutions ("Swap It"), suggested ideas for leftovers ("Double-Duty"), and given you little tips that'll help you do the job better and more efficiently ("Cowgirl Tip").

COME COOK IN MY COWGIRL KITCHEN

Trying to satiate one's hunger for home is the life of an expat. It is a life of constant longing—for the place you left, and when you return, for the place you left home for, that you thought you'd never love as your own. It's like some sort of cosmic joke. The homesickness is only lessened by the growing attachment to the new place. Then the very idea of home becomes amorphous, ever changing. Sometimes it almost feels like I'm cheating, loving both France *and* Texas.

I love them both for their food, for the passion that both places have for their cuisines. There is nothing quite like eating *enchiladas verdes* in San Antonio or bouillabaisse in Marseille. And whichever side of the Atlantic I happen to be on, I feel like I'm in a semi-constant state of withdrawal. When I'm in France, I miss the jalapeños, the serranos, and the New Mexican Hatch chiles. When I'm in Texas, I crave the French *fleur de sel* butter, the chocolate, the cheese.

Every time I'd sit down to work on this collection of recipes, I'd think about the kitchen explorations that have allowed me to bring my two beloved culinary cultures together. When you come into the kitchen to cook with me, I hope you'll discover the happiness of that fusion.

And that you'll come back often.

I've thought a lot about the kind of cookbooks I like to buy and the kind I actually use. I wanted to write something that was both practical and creative; filled with recipes that were multipurpose, could be sized up or down, or made into something else with a twist here or a trick there. And I wanted to include suggestions on what to do with a dish, how to serve it, what to pair it with, and, as much as possible, how to make it look good on the plate.

The stories I wrote alongside the recipes are meant to entertain, but first and foremost, I hope these recipes resonate. I hope they will inspire you to make them, enjoy them, and share them with your friends and family.

And, finally, I hope I've succeeded in writing a cookbook you'll dog-ear and accidentally spill your coffee on—when you're having fun cooking, that just happens. That's what cooking's all about.

What are you waiting for? So go put your boots on, and get cookin'!

CHAPTER 1

Appetizers:

OLD FAVORITES *and* NEW BEGINNINGS

Not long after I arrived in Paris, I realized that besides navigating the special driving rules of France—you always yield to traffic incoming from the right, except, of course, when you don't; only use your blinker, if at all, at that precise moment of turning the wheel, and not a second before, because where you're going is no one else's business but your own—I had a lot to learn about how the French eat.

The French dining ritual is, like many other fine traditions here, such as the twice-yearly government-sanctioned sales, fairly rigid, but once you get the hang of it, it's easy to follow along.

Dinners don't kick off the same way that they do in Texas. For example, you'd never walk into a restaurant and just start in on the red or white. And if you're at a dinner party, the same rules apply. Wine is for accompanying food. It's not for drinking yourself silly with.

Instead, you start with an aperitif, maybe open the Champagne and have a glass or two. Along with this you might have a little something to eat. Perhaps a bowl of radishes with their green ends trimmed down to a stubby "handle" length, served with a side dish of salt. Or something more elaborate, like a loaf of bread with a sausage baked right inside, served in tiny, easy-to-eat slices. Or Barbie-size quiches (see p. 54). It's all about small. You won't see a big bowl of tortillas with helpy-selfy queso served on the side.

Ahem.

Now, the importance of this course, which really isn't a course per se, but rather the prelude to the rest of the meal, cannot be overestimated. Just look at the words that are devoted to the idea of culinary foreplay in France. You've got your hors d'oeuvre, which literally means "outside of the chief work." Hors d'oeuvre is sort of the catch-all that also means "appetizer," but not in an American, buffet-style way. "Oeuvre" typically refers to a body of work, as in an artist's oeuvre; in the case of hors d'oeuvres, the word refers to the main course. As the prelude to such a main attraction, hors d'oeuvres can be little artworks in their own right. The French have canapés, one-bite little toasts topped with even smaller bits of this and that, from a quarter teaspoonful of tuna tartare to a smidgen of smoked salmon atop a wisp of crème fraîche. Shrinking things down even further, there's the amuse-bouche, also known as the amuse-gueule, meaning something to amuse your mouth. Ha! Ha! Ha!, your mouth must be thinking. Can I have some more? As if Champagne weren't amusing enough.

The truth is, I had no problem whatsoever adapting to any of this. Any evening that begins with a few glasses of Champagne is one that's getting a fine start if you ask me. And if there's something to eat along with it, all the better. But you've got to remember that Champagne is French for goodness' sake— I mean, everyone knows that—and there's no reason at all not to just go along with this very French custom of drinking Champagne and nibbling miniature food.

TEXAS KILLERS

One summer in the south of France, I was drinking chilled rosé in in the medieval town of Uzès, near Provence, and the waiter brought out the tiniest cookies I'd ever seen, no bigger than a nickel, or a 1 euro coin. They were not sweet, but savory, and because they were so small, I ate lots.

That gave me an idea. I thought, Why not come up with a spicy, cheesy cookie—something like a tortilla chip swiped through a big bowl of Rotel dip, but in the shape of the great state of Texas?

Which is what we have here.

I introduced the Texas Killers to my first cooking class students in Paris, and they were a hit. I took the savory cookies-with-a-kick to expat picnics on the Seine. I took boxes of them to X's family get-togethers, which always began with a couple of bottles of Champagne.

The Americans loved them, and, surprisingly, so did the French, including X's mother, who is so *parisienne* that she gets nervous when she has to cross the *boulevard périphérique*, the ring road that separates the city proper from the suburbs (*quelle horreur!*).

They're perfect with beer. Excellent with Champagne. And (drumroll …) the state drink of Texas, margaritas.

TEXAS KILLERS

MAKES ABOUT 9½ DOZEN TEXAS-SHAPED COOKIES

3 cups/345 grams of flour
½ teaspoon of sea salt
1½ teaspoons of sugar
¼ teaspoon of cayenne pepper
2 sticks/250 grams of butter, softened
¾ cup/55 grams of shredded cheddar cheese

1. Preheat your oven to 375°F/190°C and line a couple of cookie sheets with parchment paper.

2. Whisk together the flour, sea salt, sugar, and cayenne. In your mixer, cream the butter, then add the cheese. Now add the flour mixture and mix just until it comes together. Turn the dough out onto a lightly floured board, form two round discs, and cover them in plastic wrap. Refrigerate for a half-hour or until the dough is firm.

3. Roll out the dough and cut into Texas shapes, and put them on the cookie sheets about ½-inch/12 mm apart. Bake for about 12 minutes, or until the tips of the Panhandle just begin to brown. Let them cool on the pan.

★ **COWGIRL TIP**: Not a Texan? That's OK. You can also roll these out and simply slice and bake.

★**ADVANCE PLANNING**: These cookies freeze beautifully. They're on the fragile side, so pack them in plastic containers with layers of parchment or wax paper in between—then pull them straight from the freezer for your next party!

SWEET POTATO BISCUITS *with* HAM

There is no baguette, no croissant, no crispy, still-warm-from-the-oven *pain au chocolat* in all of France as good as my mother's biscuits. Rolled out with my grandmother's hefty wooden rolling pin with the black handles, cut out into fat circles with biscuit cutters slightly misshapen from decades of use, they are both fluffy and flaky. Slathered with butter and honey or covered with a whole bunch of gravy, so much the better—*tant mieux,* I say.

My mom only made biscuits on special occasions, and always with her fried chicken. They were not everyday food, and if they had been, I'd be as big as a double-wide. I can push back from the table from many things, but not my mom's biscuits. Ever.

This isn't her recipe, because I couldn't do justice to her biscuits, which are a proud tribute to her Birmingham, Alabama roots. Some things you just don't mess with.

I developed this recipe after tasting something similar at Doc Martin's in Taos, New Mexico. I liked the idea of marrying sweet potatoes and biscuits. So what is this recipe doing in a cowboy-boot-wearing Parisian repertoire? We've all got our soul survival foods. If I'm putting down roots anywhere for long, there must be boots and there must be biscuits.

SWEET POTATO BISCUITS WITH HAM

MAKES ABOUT 3 DOZEN (1½-INCH/4 CM) BISCUITS

1 large sweet potato (to yield 1 cup of mashed)

a big pinch of sea salt

2 cups/285 grams of flour

1½ tablespoons of baking powder

½ teaspoon of sea salt

2 tablespoons of sugar

1 stick/125 grams of butter, cut into
small cubes and chilled in the freezer

¼ cup/60 ml of milk

about 5 ounces/140 grams of thinly sliced smoked ham

1. Preheat your oven to 400°F/200°C and line a couple of cookie sheets with parchment paper.

2. Peel your sweet potatoes and cut them into fat slices, about 1-inch/2.5 cm thick. Toss them in a large, heavy stockpot, cover with cold water, and add a big pinch of sea salt. Turn the heat to high, and when the water boils, turn the fire down to a simmer and let the potatoes cook for about 5 more minutes, or until you can easily insert a fork into them—do this at the first opportunity because you don't want the potatoes to get too mushy. Drain off the water and mash up the potatoes by hand with a fork or a potato masher, making sure to leave plenty of small chunks throughout (this is what'll make the biscuits pretty!) Set this aside to cool.

3. Whisk together the flour, baking powder, sea salt, and sugar. Add the pieces of frozen butter and mix just until it looks like you've got smallish pebbles throughout. You can do this by hand, as my mom still likes to do, or use the food processor (my way).

4. Measure out 1 cup of the cooled, semi-mashed sweet potatoes, and gently mix this with ¼ cup/60 ml of milk. Now add this to the dry ingredients and mix gently, only until the dough comes together. We want pieces of sweet potato in the biscuits, so be careful not to overdo.

5. Now, the fun part. Lightly dust a work surface with flour, and roll out the dough it until it's 1-inch/2.5 cm thick. Cut out your biscuits and put them on the cookie sheets about 1-inch/2.5 cm apart. Bake for about 15 minutes, or until the edges (and the bottoms—it's OK to turn them over to check) are lightly browned. Once the biscuits are cool, split 'em open, stuff with pieces of ham, and serve.

★ **COWGIRL TIP:** Make big sweet potato biscuits instead, and serve them with soups, salads, or for breakfast—yum!

★ **SWAP IT:** Instead of ham, stuff the biscuits with: slices of Spanish chorizo or any other mildly spicy cured sausage; jalapeño pimento cheese (p.187) and fresh dill; or smoked salmon, a bit of crème fraîche, or sour cream and fresh chives.

★ **ADVANCE PLANNING:** Want hot biscuits at another time? Put your already cut-out biscuits in the freezer on the cookie sheet, and let them harden before putting them in a plastic zip-top sack. Keep them in the freezer until you're ready to bake them. Just add a couple more minutes to the baking time.

SWEET PEA PESTO

My mother only served Le Sueur brand peas, which came in small cans wrapped in shiny silver paper. They were superior to the fatter, American peas, Mom said, because they were small and delicate. They were French.

As European as they sounded, my brother and I didn't like them, and wouldn't eat them, no matter how long we had to sit at the table. After a certain pea mishap involving a double-dare and my brother's nose, peas were phased out of our family dinners.

That's how I always remembered peas. Then I moved to France and ate real French peas. Not Le Sueur. Not anything out of any sort of can. Peas so bright they were fluorescent green. Every spring, they were puréed in soups along with mint, and served, simply boiled, with fish, or chicken, or just about anything else. They were perfect.

I started buying peas by the kilo whenever they'd appear at the market, one of the first signs of spring. I loved shelling the peas in my kitchen, pulling the string, and emptying them into a handmade terra-cotta bowl from Gascony. I put peas in pasta and ate them on their own.

Now that I know the joys of fresh peas, I like them almost any way, but I like them best made into a pesto and smeared on a hunk of crusty baguette, eaten with a glass of wine or Champagne (these being French peas and all).

SWEET PEA PESTO

MAKES ABOUT 2 CUPS/480 ML

4 cups/340 grams of freshly shelled peas
  (or you may use frozen)
½ cup/30 grams of grated Parmesan cheese,
  plus more for serving
6 to 10 fresh mint leaves
1 shallot, finely chopped
1 teaspoon of olive oil
sea salt

1. Put a medium-size pot of salted water on to boil. When it's ready, drop in your peas and set the timer for 2 minutes. While the peas are cooking, fill a large bowl with ice cubes and some cold water.

2. When the timer goes off, drain the peas in a colander, and put them in the ice-water bath so they'll stay pretty and green.

3. Make your pesto. You can do this in a food processor (the easiest way) or with a hand masher. Just mix your cooled peas with the rest of the ingredients just until combined—this is meant to be coarse rather than smooth; we're not going for a purée. Pop it in the fridge for an hour to let the flavors come together. Spread this on top of toasted, thin slices of a baguette or Toasted Pita Chips (p.35) with curls of Parmesan.

★ **COWGIRL TIP:** If you're in hurry, just run some cold water over your peas instead of putting them in the ice-water bath.

★ **DOUBLE-DUTY:** Boil up your favorite chunky pasta (I love the tiny bows), and fold in this pesto. Hello, spring.

TOASTED
PITA CHIPS

A long, long time ago, when water didn't come in bottles, but straight out of the faucet, and the now-ubiquitous pita chips were still years away from being stuffed in sacks and put on the grocery store salty-snacks aisle, I learned to make my own.

It sounds so quaint and pioneer-like now.

But make them I did. I'd buy sacks of pitas, as many as two or three at a time, and with my kitchen scissors, I carefully cut each round piece of bread into quarters, and then eighths. I'd wipe my brow on my sleeve from all of the hard work, and then I'd toss the little bread triangles into a very large bowl. I wouldn't even take a break before I moved on to the next very complicated step: I'd drizzle some olive oil and sprinkle some salt and pepper over it all, and then I'd mix it up, by hand.

Then, it was onto the cookie sheet and into the hot oven, where the soft little pita pieces were magically transformed into—ta da!—crispy, salty, and peppery pita chips.

It is so old-fashioned, I know, to take the time—in this case, fifteen minutes tops, from start to finish to cut and toss and bake pita chips when you can buy them at the grocery store. Some things are just worth going that extra mile.

TOASTED PITA CHIPS

MAKES 4 DOZEN

6 pieces of pita bread*, each piece cut into eighths
about ¼ cup/60 ml of olive oil
sea salt and pepper

1. Preheat your oven to 400°F/200°C and line a couple of cookie sheets with parchment paper.

2. In a large bowl, and with your hands (it's easiest), Mix up the pita triangles with the olive oil, and a big pinch of salt and pepper. Spread these out on your cookie sheets, and cook them until they're crispy and brown, about 10 minutes; then take them out, flip them over, and cook for 5 minutes more.

* Pita bread is made two different ways—with and without a cute pocket- I always use the pocket kind.

★ **COWGIRL TIP:** For a party, simply double or triple the recipe. To save time, use your kitchen shears to cut up the pita bread.

EGGPLANT CAVIAR
(CAVIAR D'AUBERGINE)

There are no tiny, overpriced fish eggs in this "caviar"—it's actually a dip from Provence. But dip sounds about as appealing as, well, eggplant, and I think that whoever named this wonderful stuff had it right, coming up with something that sounds both elegant and unexpected, to entice us all to give it a try. As an added inducement, this caviar, like the real stuff, goes nicely with Champagne.

Eggplant caviar is another one of those things you'll find in just about every grocery store in France, next to the ready-to-eat hummus and the take-home tabouli. But I do not recommend that you try your first taste of it the pre-packaged way.

Instead, just roast up some eggplant and make your own. It's really not so hard. And there are so many fun variations—I played around a bit to come up with one that I really liked. Mine's a bit lighter and more eggplant-centric; instead of garlic, which can push every other flavor right out of the room, I lean heavily on fresh herbs.

For your next party, surprise your friends and tell them you'll bring the caviar.

EGGPLANT CAVIAR

(CAVIAR D'AUBERGINE)

MAKES ENOUGH FOR 4

2 large eggplants, halved

½ cup/120 ml of olive oil, plus a little more for
  oiling the cookie sheet

sea salt and pepper

the juice of 2 lemons

a pinch of cayenne pepper

8 fresh basil leaves, roughly torn

12 cherry tomatoes, quartered

1. Preheat your oven to 400°F/200°C and line a cookie sheet with parchment paper. Place the four halves of eggplant on this, insides-up, and with a sharp knife, make a few long slashes into the flesh of each one. Brush the olive oil on your eggplant pieces, making sure to use it all—the eggplant should willingly soak it right up. A sprinkle of salt and pepper, and into the oven they go. Bake for 45 minutes to 1 hour, until the eggplant halves are soft and the tops have browned. Remove from the oven and let cool.

2. Scoop out the eggplant's flesh and mix it up—in your food processor or simply with a fork, if you like it chunky—with the lemon juice, cayenne, and basil. Taste for seasonings, then gently fold in the cherry tomato quarters. Refrigerate for an hour before serving.

> ★ **DOUBLE-DUTY:** Make eggplant caviar tartines. Toast some bread, spread it with this delicious stuff, and add some more basil and a drizzle of olive oil.

BASIL PESTO MATCHSTICKS
(PESTO ALLUMETTES)

Some people look forward to sleeping in on Saturday mornings. I am not one of those people.

I think the best place to be at 7:30 in Paris on a Saturday morning is at the Porte de Vanves flea market, a year-round, weekend junk sale with vendors who back up their vans to a long stretch of sidewalk, and unload their booty onto folding tables and right onto the ground, in cardboard boxes. The sellers are never the same from week to week, so you never know what treasures you might find.

I once scored an enormous copper stockpot, in perfect condition, for 40 euros. I've bought vintage silverware for 1 euro a stem. I've picked up oversize antique French linen kitchen towels known as *torchons*, hand-stitched with the initials of the former owner in red. An Eiffel Tower bottle opener, a carving knife with the leg of a deer as a handle, blue and white café au lait bowls—the finds are endless.

It is best to go early, as anyone who loves fleas knows. Early affords a clearer view of the merchandise, without the crowds of like-minded people who show up at around 9, lit cigarettes in hand, held at waist-level, dogs in tow, pushing baby strollers, and unbelievably, sometimes all three.

I wake up, throw back a small, strong coffee like a shot of tequila, and I'm out the door. Thirty minutes and two changes on the metro later, I'm there, with an empty bag thrown on my shoulder, and a few euros in my pocket. I shop fast, and with an air of detachment. I never make the first offer, letting the seller do the bargaining instead, and I am always ready to walk away. I usually get what I want, and for the right price.

Afterward, on the short walk back to the metro, I stop into a boulangerie and buy an *allumette choco-noisette*, which is basically a long strip of croissant dough filled with Nutella. Then I take it to the café next door and order an extra-hot café au lait to celebrate my good luck—whether I found something or not—to be living in Paris and spending a Saturday morning just like this.

BASIL PESTO MATCHSTICKS
(PESTO ALLUMETTES)

MAKES ABOUT 4 DOZEN

1 cup/200 grams of ricotta cheese
$1\frac{1}{4}$ sticks/180 grams of butter, softened
$2\frac{1}{4}$ cups/285 grams of flour
$\frac{1}{2}$ teaspoon of sea salt
Basil Pesto (recipe follows), or you may use store-bought
1 egg white, mixed with a little water

1. Preheat your oven to 400°F/200°C and line two cookie sheets with parchment paper.

2. Whip the butter with the ricotta until it's light and fluffy. Add the flour and salt and mix until it forms a solid mass. Wrap the dough in plastic and pop it into the fridge for a half-hour.

3. To make the matchsticks, divide your dough in half, and put one half on a lightly floured surface, and the other back in the fridge to stay cool. Roll out your dough into a large rectangle. Spread a couple of tablespoons of pesto on one half of the dough, then fold over the other half. Using a pizza cutter, cut the dough into strips $\frac{1}{2}$-inch by 5-inches/12 mm by 12 cm wide, and lay each piece on one of the cookie sheets, leaving about a $\frac{1}{4}$ inch/6 mm between each one.

4. Brush a little egg white mixed with water on each strip, and slide the first pan into the oven for 20 minutes, or until the matchsticks are light brown. Repeat the above step with the second half of the dough. Serve warm or at room temperature.

★ **COWGIRL TIP:** Keep uneaten matchsticks in the fridge and simply reheat by putting directly on a cookie sheet and popping back into the oven (400°F/200°C) for 10 minutes—they'll crisp right back up.

★ **SWAP IT:** Instead of Basil Pesto, use Kalamata Olive-Basil Salsa (p.269), or go the sweet route, and spread these with Nutella, your favorite jam, or cinnamon and sugar.

BASIL PESTO
MAKES ABOUT 1 CUP/240 ML

¼ cup/35 grams of toasted pine nuts
a big handful of fresh basil (about 2 packed cups, or
  enough to completely fill a small food processor)
3 tablespoons of olive oil
1 clove of garlic, minced
¼ cup/15 grams of grated Parmesan cheese
sea salt and pepper

Toss the pine nuts in your small food processor and pulse until they're roughly chopped. Now, add the basil and pack it in as tight as you can. Pour in the olive oil and pulse until the basil is nice and fine; then toss in your minced garlic clove, Parmesan, and big pinch of salt and pepper. Taste.

★ **DOUBLE-DUTY:**

• Spread your pesto on the bottom of a tart, such as the Tomato-Ricotta Tart (p.172)

• Smear some Basil Pesto on a split, toasted baguette, add chopped tomatoes and mozzarella for a super-quick pizza.

• Stuff it under the skin of your Easy Roast Chicken (p.265).

MUSHROOM TAPENADE

In France, the mushroom population is so vast and varied that pharmacists are required to have a working knowledge of the different varieties, so they'll know, for instance, if you've been out foraging in the forest and have filled up your cute wicker mushroom basket, that you've plucked the very delicious, edible kind, and not the poisonous Shakespearean, kill-your-enemy ones.

As someone who grew up eating mushrooms from cans (fresh mushrooms weren't yet available at the Piggly Wiggly) I still get overwhelmed when I go to the market and see the endless selection of mushrooms. It seems odd, foreign, and exotic. There's even a stand at Marché Avenue du Président Wilson (President Wilson market in the 16th arrondissement) that, along with potatoes, sells only mushrooms, from the oversize, prized *cèpes* (porcini) in the fall to the pricey *morilles* (morels) in the spring, along with gangly-legged *girolles,* blue-hued *pieds bleus* from Brittany, shitakes, and delicate triangle-topped *mousserons*, which look the most fairylike of all.

But no need to get overly fancy. My everyday go-to mushroom is the most common of all—*le champignon de Paris,* a.k.a. the white button. It does, however, have a most uncommon history.

At the turn of the nineteenth century, France, much like my hometown Piggly Wiggly in the 1970s, didn't have these mushrooms, and was either making do without or taking its chances with the often-chancy forest fungi.

But all of that changed in the mid-1800s, when Napoleon III hired Baron Haussmann to modernize Paris, then still a smelly old medieval city, with narrow streets and buildings that were in need of repair. Since the city's center had already been quarried to such a degree that it had fallen in on itself a few times, Haussmann had limestone hauled in from the suburbs.

Imagine the baron's surprise when he found hundreds of beautiful, crisp white mushrooms growing on the rocks brought in to rebuild the capital—which is how these mushrooms, still grown in a mixture of dirt and manure in caves just outside of the *périphérique*, became known as the mushrooms of Paris.

MUSHROOM TAPENADE

MAKES ENOUGH FOR ABOUT 20 LITTLE BAGUETTE TOASTS

about 2 tablespoons of olive oil

about 2 tablespoons of butter

2 shallots, finely chopped

16 ounces/450 grams of white mushrooms, chopped

a few sprigs of fresh thyme, leaves removed,
    plus more for serving

5 ounces/150 grams of soft goat cheese

1 baguette, thinly sliced and toasted

1. Put 1 tablespoon of olive oil and 1 tablespoon of butter along with the shallots in your largest skillet, and turn your heat to medium. When the butter melts, add as many mushrooms as will comfortably fit, leaving a little space between them so they can brown—if you've got too many mushrooms in the pan, they'll steam and become soggy, which we don't want. To prevent this, I usually cook them in batches, adding equal amounts of olive oil and butter with each batch. Salt and pepper as you go, then put the cooked mushrooms in a bowl to cool.

2. Toss your cooled mushrooms with the fresh thyme. Spread a bit of goat cheese on your little toasts, add a spoonful of mushrooms, and a drizzle of olive oil. Lay these out on a platter and sprinkle with more fresh thyme.

> ★ **DOUBLE-DUTY:** You can also stir your mushrooms into an omelette, put them on a pizza, add them to pasta with lots of Pecorino-Romano, or stuff them into a baked potato.

CHICKEN EMPANADAS *with* CILANTRO YOGURT

I bit into my first empanada one afternoon in Miami at a stand-up Cuban coffee bar in South Beach. I was about to set sail on a country music cruise that even Lyle Lovett couldn't rescue from sinking, and I had no idea that I was about to have my last edible nosh for days. The empanada was no longer warm, but the *café con leche* was hot and strong, and between the two, my hazy sun-soaked world came back into focus.

What I liked about the empanada was its familiar half-moon fried-pie shape. Like a fried pie, it was easily eaten with one hand and carried from here to there. The dough was flaky, yet sturdy enough to fold over and not fall apart in your hands. It tasted great, and it was practical, which you can't say about many crusts.

Back in Paris on terra firma, I started tinkering around with doughs and fillings. I made these cute little chicken empanadas and took them to a meeting where my cowgirled-up version of the Latin American standby was such a big hit I knew I was onto something.

CHICKEN EMPANADAS WITH CILANTRO YOGURT

MAKES ABOUT 4 DOZEN

2¼ cups/300 grams of flour

1 teaspoon of sea salt

1 stick/125 grams of butter, cut into small pieces and popped in the freezer ahead of time

2 eggs

⅓ cup/75 ml of ice water (or a little less)

1 tablespoon of white vinegar

canola oil

1 onion, diced

2 cloves of garlic, minced

2 cups/345 grams of cooked, shredded chicken (use leftover Easy Roast Chicken, p.265)

1 roasted red bell pepper (p.185), diced or you may use store-bought

½ teaspoon of cumin

¼ teaspoon of cayenne pepper

Cilantro Yogurt (recipe follows)

1. First, make your dough. Whisk together your flour and salt. Add the pieces of cold butter and either with a pastry cutter or pulsing in a food processor, cut in the butter only until the mixture resembles coarse meal with small pieces that look like pebbles.

2. Whisk one of the eggs with the water and vinegar in a small bowl. Add this to flour mixture, and blend just until the wet and dry ingredients are incorporated, but it's still a bit crumbly—you don't want to overmix. Dump the dough directly onto a piece of plastic wrap, and form your dough into a disc. Refrigerate for an hour.

3. While the dough's chilling, you can make your filling. Put a little canola oil into a large skillet, along with the onion and garlic, and turn the heat to medium-low. Cook for a few minutes, just until the onions become translucent. Now add your shredded chicken, diced red bell pepper, cumin, cayenne, and pinch of sea salt. Stir it up, reduce the heat to low, and after about 10 minutes, turn off the heat. Let the chicken cool completely before you stuff the empanadas.

4. When you're ready to make your empanadas, preheat your oven to 375°F/190°C and line a couple of cookie sheets with parchment paper. Roll out your dough, and using a biscuit cutter, cut out 3¼-inch (8.5 cm) circles, and place these on the cookie sheets. Stuff them with a spoonful of chicken, fold the dough over, and press the edges together with the tines of a fork. Whisk the second egg with a little water and brush this over your dough, especially around the edges to seal it together. Cook for about 10 minutes or until the edges begin to brown—at this point, you can also freeze the empanadas and simply reheat them later for about 25 minutes at the same temperature.

CILANTRO YOGURT
MAKES ABOUT 1½ CUPS/300 GRAMS

1¼ cup /300 grams of Greek yogurt
a small handful of fresh cilantro, chopped
about 1 tablespoon of chopped fresh chives
1 clove of garlic, minced
the juice of 1 lime
a pinch of cumin
a pinch of cayenne pepper
sea salt

Mix everything together in a small bowl and refrigerate for an hour. Taste again before serving and adjust any seasonings.

CHEESY ROSEMARY-OLIVE FLATBREAD

Sometimes on Sundays, X, my Australian shepherd, Rose, and I hop in the car and drive to the Louveciennes forest near Versailles for a long morning walk. There are trails over hills and through dense trees and open spaces, which I like, and plenty of sticks to be thrown and fetched, which Rose likes. As much fun as it is tromping through Louis XIV's old hunting grounds, the real reason I love going to Versailles is the *fougasse* at the Maison Guinon boulangerie, where they bake bread the same way they have since 1802. The line is always out the door, snaking down the sidewalk, but the wait is worth it.

Walking always makes me hungry for wheat-shaped bread stuffed with olives and cheese. And this Provençal take on Italian focaccia is such an easy and satisfying snack. I love tearing it apart with my hands and sharing a hunk on the way to the Sunday market down the street. The Versailles market— an indoor/outdoor setup with permanent fish, meat, spice, and vegetable vendors in four different long buildings in what were once the royal stables—has been the scene of much aisle-meandering and *fougasse* devouring.

I love stuffing myself on bread, but my jeans (which have some stretch, but not nearly enough) do not. So, with cheese, olives, and looser-fitting jeans in mind, I made a version without yeast, flattened it out, and created this very quick and easy flatbread inspired by my very favorite, very bready *fougasse*.

Like the *fougasse,* this is also perfect for tearing and sharing.

CHEESY ROSEMARY-
OLIVE FLATBREAD

MAKES 4 FLATBREADS, ENOUGH FOR 8 PEOPLE

2½ cups/300 grams of flour, plus a bit more
   for dusting the pan and shaping the dough

1½ teaspoons of baking powder

½ teaspoon of sea salt

2 tablespoons of chopped fresh rosemary

1½ cups/160 grams of grated cheddar cheese

5 ounces/150 ml of water

2 tablespoons of olive oil, plus a bit more for
   brushing on top of the flatbreads

a handful (about 20) of pitted kalamata olives,
   roughly chopped

1. Position a rack in the lowest part of your oven and preheat it to
   450°F/230°C. Line a large cookie sheet with parchment paper.

2. Whisk together your flour, baking powder, salt, and rosemary. Add the
   cheese, water, and olive oil, and with your hands or a mixer—it'll work
   either way—and mix it all together until it's a nice smooth dough.

3. Divide the dough into 4 pieces, take out one piece, and cover up the rest
   with plastic wrap so it'll stay moist. Flatten the first piece of dough with
   your hand, and put about one-quarter of the chopped olives on top. Fold
   the dough over itself, like you're closing a book, and put it onto your
   parchment-lined cookie sheet. With your hands or rolling pin—I use
   both—very gently press out the dough until it's a thin, long, football
   shape. Repeat with the remaining dough pieces. Brush the tops of the
   flatbreads with a little more olive oil, and pop them in the oven. Cook for
   15 minutes or until they're brown and crispy. Serve warm—these are
   great straight from the oven, although they're fine at room temperature,
   too.

To reheat your flatbreads: Just pop them into the oven at 450°F/230°C for about 10 minutes—or if you're impatient like me, just tear off pieces and put them in the toaster—works like a charm.

> ★ **COWGIRL TIP:** Rosemary is one of the easiest herbs to grow; I always have some in my garden—in a clay pot or right in the ground.
>
> ★ **SWAP IT:** Instead of cheddar, try Parmesan, Gorgonzola, or Roquefort. Nix the olives and add bits of ham instead.

TINY TARTS

The French are as obsessed with making things small as Americans are with super-sizing them.

Like cars, some of which are only slightly bigger than Rose's doghouse. Appliances, such as my Barbie-size stove, which can bake no more than twelve cookies at a time. Apartments and bathrooms, especially, with rectangular sinks no bigger than a ballet slipper box. There are miniature magazines and tiny Rhodia notepads no more than two inches wide by three inches tall, with tiny pens to write on them with.

Then there's the whole idea of miniaturized food. Pass by any boulangerie or patisserie and you'll see the classics, downsized: pinky-size éclairs stuffed with chocolate and coffee-flavored pastry cream; lemon meringue tarts that'll fit in the palm of your hand; *pains au chocolat*, croissants, the French apple turnover called *chausson aux pommes* that you can eat by the handful; and the cutest damn quiches you've ever seen.

I have never been to a cocktail party in Paris and not been served baby quiches. To the French, I suspect these two-bite quiches are simply familiar, smaller versions of what they eat all the time. I don't think they find them fancy or particularly elegant. But I do.

TINY TARTS

MAKES 30 BITE-SIZED TARTS

CRUST

2¼ cups/300 grams of flour

½ teaspoon of sea salt

1 stick/125 grams of butter, cut into tiny pieces
  and put in the freezer ahead of time

1 egg, separated

about ½ cup/120 ml of ice water

FILLING

2 eggs

½ cup/120 ml of milk

a big pinch of nutmeg

sea salt and pepper

1 to 2 tablespoons of diced green chile
  (I use canned in France)

1 to 2 tablespoons of goat cheese

1 to 2 tablespoons of Mushroom Tapenade (p.43)

1 to 2 tablespoons of crumbled feta

1 to 2 tablespoons of diced ham

1 to 2 tablespoons of diced Swiss cheese

1. Preheat the oven to 375°F/190°C and get out your nonstick mini-muffin
pan.

2. Make the dough for the crust by first whisking together the flour and the
salt. Working quickly, either with a pastry cutter or pulsing in a food
processor, cut in the butter only until it looks like small pebbles (if you
work this until it's uniform, the butter will get too warm and your dough
won't puff).

3. Whisk your egg yolk with 2 tablespoons of the ice water, then sprinkle this on top of your flour-butter mixture. Quickly incorporate this, and then add just enough additional water—I use the "sprinkle 2 to 3 tablespoons at a time" method—for the dough to come together when you press it between your fingers. It should look crumbly. Dump the dough onto a piece of plastic wrap, mash it into a round disk, then wrap tightly and put it in the fridge for an hour.

4. When the dough's firm, take it out and put it on your floured work surface. Roll out your dough, and cut out round pieces just slightly bigger than the size of the muffin mold, and very gently press each little piece of dough into each one. Once you've filled up your tin, slide this in the freezer for 15 minutes or the fridge for about 30, or until the dough is firm (it's very important for dough to be firm so it won't fall in on itself when you get to the next step).

5. Half-bake your little crusts. Brush the dough with the egg white mixed with a little water, and pop into the oven for 15 to 20 minutes, or until the crusts turn a light brown.

6. Make your filling: Mix up the eggs, milk, nutmeg, sea salt, and pepper.

7. Now, you've got a choice. You can make all ham and Swiss, mushroom and Feta, or green chile and goat cheese quiches—it's up to you. Just know that you need to put only the tiniest amount of ingredients in the little tart shells, just enough for a taste, because you need to leave room to pour the egg mixture on top. Go with less than you think that you need, and it'll probably be just right. Put your tiny tarts back in the oven and bake for 15 to 20 minutes or until the custard is set. Serve warm or at room temperature—these are great either way—and don't forget the Champagne.

CHAPTER 2

Cowgirlified Frenchy

For most of my life, I put jalapeños on or in just about every-thing I ate. On pizzas and cheeseburgers. Chopped up and stirred into pasta sauces, gumbos, and soups. In scrambled eggs and with beans of all types. I bought them fresh and pickled, sliced and whole. My father grew jalapeños and canned them himself and always sent me home with a half-dozen or so jars at the end of each summer.

Then I moved to Paris. Where there were no jalapeños. I just couldn't get over this.

To fill in the American gap in my cupboards, I brought suitcases stuffed with staples from Texas back to Paris every few months, but I was always running out of something. A Samsonite, no matter how big, will only hold so many cans of jalapeños, so much Velveeta. At some point, your Reese's disappear, there's no more Rotel, and you're down to your last Frito. So, I figured that perhaps I needed to try to adapt, and at least be open to the idea that maybe there were some things that I needed to learn in my new country.

It wasn't that I didn't love French food. Besides making crêpes and the occasional crème brûlée, I just had not ventured very far into French cuisine. Like many people, I thought it was complicated and intimidating. But the longer I lived here, the more I realized that French food wasn't either of those things. It was just unfamiliar.

Once I became determined to learn, I began to see similarities instead of differences. The onion-bell pepper mixture known as *piperade* in the Pays Basque reminded me of the onions and peppers that always come with fajitas back home. The buttery *quatre-quart* cakes (p.279) in boulangeries all over the country were a like the pound cakes of my childhood. The more I could relate the foreign to the familiar, the more comfortable I got. And then a funny thing happened: I became more interested in what was right in front of me than in what I'd left behind.

When I'd go to restaurants, I started asking the chefs how to make what I'd just eaten, from *brandade*-stuffed *piquillo* peppers in Biarritz to a *noisette* (hazelnut) crème brûlée in Honfleur to the Roquefort sauce (p.243) with the steak frîtes at my favorite bistro in the 17th arrondissement. They were all happy to let me into their kitchens, and each patiently showed me how.

I started to make these new recipes, and they turned out surprisingly well. I began reading the French cooking magazines each month, tearing out pages of recipes I wanted to try. My French — or at least the words and phrases that dealt with cooking — improved. I bought tart pans and French cookbooks — in French. I made monthly runs to G. Detou, the city's professional pastry supply shop in Les Halles, for vanilla, baking chocolate, hazelnuts, and almonds, all of which I started buying in bulk.

Connecting with the food helped me to connect with the place. I no longer felt like an outsider.

At some point, I felt confident enough to take French recipes and techniques and make them my own. Keep the original intention, and arrive at the same destination, but take it down a different road. It didn't happen overnight, this merging of what I was most comfortable with—Tex-Mex and Southern home cooking—with French cuisine, but once it did, there was no turning back. Suddenly, I saw possibilities everywhere.

I call it Cowgirlified Frenchy. A little bit me, a little bit them.

COWGIRL QUICHE

"This," I said excitedly to X after I took my first bite, "is just like a breakfast taco!"

I felt like I'd hit the jackpot, told Carol Merrill to pick the right door, and was about to go home with the prize money *and* the new side-by-side. I could hardly contain myself.

"Isn't it *just like a breakfast taco?*" I said, again, trying to elicit a response.

X looked at me, puzzled. "Breakfast? Taco?"

"Breakfast taco," I said. "Scrambled eggs, chorizo, and maybe some cheese or potatoes, wrapped up in a flour tortilla?"

"For breakfast?"

"All right," I said. "Imagine having too much tequila the night before. Too many margaritas, let's say. The next morning, what would you want to eat?"

"I don't like margaritas," he said.

This is how it goes with us. We are forever lost in translation, having to overexplain things that you just breeze through with people who know you, who come from where you come from.

So you'll just have to take my word for it: This quiche is just like a great hangover breakfast taco. X, for the record, loves it, even though he doesn't really understand why.

COWGIRL QUICHE

MAKES ONE (11-INCH/28 CM) TART

1 half-baked Polenta Tart Crust (p.183)
1 cup/65 grams of grated cheddar cheese
1½ cups/170 grams of crumbled Cowgirl Chorizo (p.322)
1 (4.5 ounce/127 gram) can of chopped green chile
3 eggs
½ cup/120 ml of milk
½ cup/120 ml of cream
sea salt and pepper
fresh chives

1. Preheat your oven to 400°F/200°C and put your half-baked Polenta Tart Crust on a foil-lined cookie sheet.

2. Scatter the grated cheddar, chorizo, and green chile on the bottom of your crust.

3. Beat the eggs with the milk, cream, and good pinch of salt and pepper. Gently pour the eggy mixture over the cheese, chorizo, and green chile, and snip some fresh chives all over the top. Bake for 30 to 40 minutes, or until set—you'll know it's done when the edges begin to puff. Serve warm or at room temperature.

★ **COWGIRL TIP:** I always bake my tarts on cookie sheets lined with foil to catch any eggy drips in case of tart pans with leaky bottoms. As a secondary measure, I'll often wrap the bottom of my tart pan with foil, too. This may sound like overkill, but I really hate scrubbing baked-on eggs off of pans.

★ **LEFTOVERS?** Just cut into pieces, wrap in foil, and pop into the freezer. To reheat, preheat oven to 400°F/200°C, unwrap the top of the foil so heat can get to the tart pieces, and place directly on the rack in the oven. Should take 35 to 45 minutes.

CORNBREAD MADELEINES

I have a thing for seashells.

I've got seashells in bowls all over our Paris apartment—smooth yellow ones from Indonesia; thick, alabaster ones from Thailand; hefty deeply grooved charcoal gray ones from the beaches of Normandy; and delicate sand dollars from Port Aransas, Texas, where my beachcombing began.

Every summer, my mom, dad, brother, and I would pile into our Buick station wagon and drive eight hours south on I-35 for seven days of sunburns and blistering hot sand. A week of early mornings that started with cinnamon bear claws from the Island Bakery and walks on the beach, to pick over the tide's just-washed-in seashells clinging to the wet shore. We'd all set out in different directions, combing that sweet spot between the outline of sea foam and the water's edge, seeking the best treasures.

After a few hours, we'd go back to the Tropic Island motel, where Mom would make sandwiches in the kitchenette with fresh-baked Island Bakery bread and thick slices of peppery German sausage and spicy mustard that we'd bought at the New Braunfels Smokehouse along the way.

I bought my first madeleine pan in Paris because it reminded me of seashells and Port Aransas. And the first thing that I made wasn't traditional madeleine cakes, but my mom's cornbread—a nod to my Southern roots and my new French home.

CORNBREAD MADELEINES

MAKES 24

4 tablespoons of bacon drippings or butter
2 cups/285 grams of cornmeal
½ cup/80 grams of flour
2 teaspoons of baking powder
½ teaspoon of baking soda
½ teaspoon of sea salt
2 eggs, lightly beaten
2 cups/480 ml of buttermilk

1. Preheat your oven to 400°F/200°C.

2. When the oven's hot, divide the bacon drippings (or butter, depending on which way you go) among the 24 madeleine molds (you'll need 2 pans with 12 molds each) and slide into the oven so the pan gets nice and hot. Depending on the size of your oven, you may need to do this one pan at a time, and bake your madeleines in batches.

3. Whisk together the cornmeal, flour, baking powder, baking soda, and salt. Combine the lightly beaten eggs with the buttermilk, and mix this into the dry ingredients. Pull your hot pans out of the oven, pour the bacon grease or butter into the batter, give it a quick stir, and divide the batter among the madeleine molds. Bake for 25 to 30 minutes or until lightly browned. Pull them from the oven and remove immediately by giving the pan a bang on your countertop—they'll pop right out.

★ **COWGIRL TIP:** If you don't have a madeleine pan, don't worry. Just use your muffin pan instead.

★ **DOUBLE-DUTY:** Leftover cornbread? Make croutons. Cut the cornbread pieces into cubes, toss them on a cookie sheet and pop into a 400°F/200°C oven for 15-20 minutes or until crispy.

★ **GREAT WITH:** Soups (p. 83), Texas Chili (p.320), and Salads (p.117).

SLICE *and* BAKE HAZELNUT-CHOCOLATE CHIP COOKIES

You live in another country and you start to notice that they just don't do things the way they do back home. They talk funny. They drink tiny, strong, and often sugary coffees, thrown back in two sips, while standing at the bar; or else big milky ones, served in bowls, in the morning. They don't eat in the car; instead, they stop somewhere and sit down and *have lunch*. They aren't big snackers.

And their cookies … well, they aren't like the ones I was used to craving.

I'm forever saying to X around 3 or 4 in the afternoon, "I sure wish I had some cookies," because this is the time that I usually have a big and not-so-milky coffee, and what goes better with that than cookies?

"Hmmpf," he says, if he responds at all.

Yes, they have cookies in France and they have a cookie aisle per se in their grocery stores, but they're called biscuits, not cookies, so already, it's not the same thing. Look closer and you'll see a clue. Written across many of the biscuit boxes and bags is *"Petit Déjeuner,"* meaning "breakfast."

Breakfast cookies. Not that I have a problem with that.

The preferred cookie in France is something called a *sablé,* which means sandy, referring to the cookie's texture. Buttery shortbread cookies, basically. Again, no problems here.

But when I say that I want a cookie, what I really want is an American chocolate chip cookie, or even better, a peanut butter-chocolate chip. Or at least, that's what I used to mean.

Live long enough in another country and the line between us and them begins to blur. You begin to adapt. You find that you love the French peanut, *la noisette,* or hazelnut, as much as peanuts themselves. You seek out hazelnut-flavored anything you can get your hands on, from cakes called "the Russian" to chocolates and pastries with creamy, crunchy hazelnut middles. You have a deeper appreciation of the Italian Nutella, the perfect marriage of chocolate and hazelnuts. Then it happens. Peanut-chocolate cravings are replaced with hazelnut-chocolate cravings, and even cookies take on a French accent.

Which brings us to this little cookie that I now crave in the afternoons, a French version of my American favorite. It's a *sablé*, but it's loaded with nuts and chocolate chips, and comes together in a very American slice-and-bake format.

As difficult as some French-American alliances can be, this one totally works.

SLICE AND BAKE HAZELNUT-CHOCOLATE CHIP COOKIES

MAKES 2 DOZEN

½ cup/70 grams of hazelnuts

¼ cups/160 grams of flour

1 teaspoon of baking soda

½ teaspoon of sea salt

1 stick/125 grams of butter, softened

¼ cup/55 grams of sugar

¼ cup/55 grams of brown sugar

1 teaspoon of vanilla extract

½ cup/80 grams of mini chocolate chips

1. Toast your hazelnuts by tossing them in a heavy skillet over low heat. This won't take long, so watch them carefully and shake the pan around every now and then so all sides get toasted. When you can smell them, and see that the skins are starting to lift away, pour the hazelnuts onto a clean dishtowel laid out flat on the countertop, and use the towel to rub the skins off. Don't worry if small bits of skin stick to some of the nuts; this is fine. When the nuts are cool, chop them up to a mixture that's about half fine, and half still chunky—you can use the food processor for this, but just be sure not to overdo (they'll quickly turn to powder, and we want both small- and medium-size pieces).

2. Sift together the flour, baking soda, and salt. In your mixer, beat the butter until it's light and fluffy; then add the sugars and vanilla and mix well. Add your flour mixture, and combine only until it comes together—err on the side of crumbly, because you're not finished yet.

3. Fold in the toasted, chopped hazelnuts and chocolate chips by hand. Don't worry if the dough still seems too crumbly; like tart dough, it'll come together while it's chilling down. Divide the dough in half and shape each piece into a 12-inch/31 cm log—I usually roll mine to be about 2 inches/5 cm in diameter. Wrap the logs in plastic wrap and pop in the fridge for an hour, or until firm.

4. To bake your cookies, preheat the oven to 375° F/190°C and line the baking sheets with parchment paper. Slice the cookies into pieces 1/4 inch/6 mm thick, and put them on the baking sheets, leaving about 1 inch/2.5 cm between each cookie. Bake for around 14 minutes, just until the cookies begin to firm around the edges. You don't want them to get brown; if they do, they'll be too hard when they cool. Let the cookies cool right on the pan. These are meant to be eaten once they're cool, but I can never resist eating them warm, too—I'm an equal opportunity cookie eater.

★ **COWGIRL TIP:** A plastic bag and a rolling pin makes a fine "nut chopper," too.

PEANUT BUTTER-CHOCOLATE SOUFFLÉS

I always thought soufflés were as fussy as the French—too delicate, too froufrou, and certainly not worth the trouble.

Then one day, I slipped into the booth at Bistrot Paul Bert, one of Paris' great old-school bistros, and ordered some wine.

For lunch. So, as you can see, I was already heading to the other side.

On this particular crispy fall afternoon, I had a kink in my back and was in desperate need of a new hairdo. X, wanting to please, offered to take me to lunch, so off on Nadine, his mauve-colored scooter, we went. Which is how I landed at Bistrot Paul Bert in the first place, and why I decided to order the chocolate soufflé. The Frenchiest, fluffiest dessert of all.

It was divine to the 100th power. Each bite a puffy, warm chocolate cloud, with a crunchy sugar-rimmed crust. I forgot about my woes with all of that goodness, every last bit of it, just for me. Other than one bite, I did not share.

Naturally, I soon tried my hand at chocolate soufflés. I got out my ramekins and dusted the insides with sugar for that Bistrot Paul Bert crunch. I whipped up some egg whites. I folded them into chocolate. When I pulled my most-perfect soufflés from the oven and took that first bite, I felt so silly for my former anti-soufflé sentiments.

It was a gateway soufflé, which naturally led me down a path of soufflé experimentation, and the uncontrollable binge buying of eggs. Which is how I came up with this, a soufflé that tastes like an inside-out Reese's, sacks of which I always stuff into my suitcase to take back to Paris, and keep in the freezer in case of emergencies.

PEANUT BUTTER-CHOCOLATE SOUFFLÉS

MAKES 6

butter, for buttering the ramekins

4 ounces/100 grams of good-quality white chocolate

³⁄₄ cup/180 ml of cream

3 tablespoons of smooth peanut butter (I like Skippy, because that's all that's available in Paris, but I'd steer clear of natural peanut butters for this)

1 teaspoon of vanilla extract

3 egg yolks, at room temperature

4 egg whites, at room temperature

3 tablespoons of sugar, plus more for dusting the ramekins

¹⁄₄ cup/55 grams of semisweet or a good milk chocolate, chopped

1. Preheat your oven to 400°F/200°C and butter the insides of six ¹⁄₂ cup/ 115-gram ramekins and dust with sugar.

2. Melt the white chocolate, cream, and peanut butter in the top of a double boiler over simmering water. Remove from the heat, add the vanilla, and let this cool.

3. When the peanut butter-white chocolate mixture has cooled a bit, whisk in the egg yolks.

4. In your mixer (and using a super-clean bowl—egg whites are notoriously finicky), whip the egg whites on high speed until they start to hold their shape. Now add the sugar, and whip until soft peaks form.

5. Using your biggest rubber spatula, gently fold the egg whites into the peanut butter mixture, mixing them in in 3 additions. Don't worry if it's a bit streaky—this is much better than overmixing, which will lessen your soufflés' puffy tops.

6. Fill the ramekins halfway with the soufflé batter, and sprinkle some the chopped chocolate bits on top. Now, add the rest of the batter, filling each ramekin almost to the top. Put these on a parchment-lined cookie sheet and gently slide them into the oven.

5. Bake for about 15 minutes, or just until the soufflés rise and puff (they'll look like they've gotten cute little hats) and begin to crack across the top. Don't be in a rush to take these from the oven at the first opportunity—you want these to be firm (not runny) throughout, so just let them bake. Serve your perfect soufflés immediately.

> ★ **COWGIRL TIP:** Don't have a double boiler? Neither do I. I simply put a glass bowl over a deep saucepan filled with just enough water to warm the bowl, but not touch the bottom. Works like a charm.

PARIS CHICKEN FRICASSÉE

X and I had been fighting all afternoon. By dinnertime, it was time for a truce, which is how things usually go with us. No matter what we've disagreed over, by dinnertime, we break the silence and we start talking again, even if it's just about whether we want to order in a pizza or go out. We sit down across the table from each other and we eat.

Eating together is always been a way for us to reconnect.

On this particular fall evening, we set out for a walk in Saint-Germain, crossed over to the Right Bank, and meandered back into the Marais, crisscrossing the narrow cobblestone streets, not knowing where we were going, and not saying much as we were walking, either. I still wasn't that familiar with Paris, and I had no ideas about where we could go. After we'd walked for more than an hour, I got hungry and my feet were tired. X told me to hop on his back, and for the next block or two he gave me a piggyback ride.

Yes, a piggyback ride.

We soon found a simple bistro, Vin des Pyrénées, and I hopped off.

I ordered fish, and he ordered chicken *fricassée,* which is an elegant, Frenchy way of vaguely saying "cooked in a sauce." When his dish arrived, I knew I'd ordered the wrong thing. His chicken came in a cute black cast-iron pot; when he lifted the lid, I smelled rosemary and saw chicken thighs and fat pieces of Spanish chorizo in a tomato sauce. He offered me a bite, which I happily took, and then we traded. It was impossible to stay mad at him after that.

PARIS CHICKEN FRICASSÉE

MAKES 4 SERVINGS

4 chicken legs with the thighs attached

½ cup/50 grams of flour

1 teaspoon each of sea salt and pepper

1 (32-ounce/765 gram) can of whole tomatoes

olive oil

1 onion, sliced into half-moons

1 clove of garlic, minced

a few sprigs of fresh rosemary, leaves removed and
chopped, plus a bit more for serving

5 ounces/150 grams of cooked and crumbled Cowgirl
Chorizo (p.322), or you may use store-bought

½ of a habañero pepper, finely chopped (if you dare)

1. Rinse and pat your chicken pieces dry with a paper towel and set them aside.

2. Mix together your flour, salt, and pepper in a plastic bag by giving it a shake. Now, put one piece of chicken at a time in the sack and shake like crazy, so it's well coated. Reach in, shake off the excess flour, and put the chicken on a plate. Do the same thing with the rest of the chicken pieces.

3. Pour your tomatoes into a medium bowl and tear them up with your hands.

4. Drizzle a little olive oil in your biggest skillet (large enough to hold all of the chicken pieces), and turn the heat to medium. When it's hot, add the chicken legs, skin-side down, and let them cook for just 4 to 5 minutes, until they're brown and crispy. Now flip them over to the other side. It'll just take another 3 minutes or so. Remove your chicken legs and let them rest on the plate while you make the sauce.

5. Reduce the heat to medium-low, add your onions, and start scraping the bottom of the pan to remove the browned bits. After a minute or so, the

onions will slightly soften. Now, add your garlic and let it cook for about a minute, just until you can smell it.

6. Turn your heat down again; this time to the lowest setting. Add the tomatoes and their juices to the skillet, and give it a stir. Toss in about 1 tablespoon of the fresh chopped rosemary, the chorizo, and your finely minced habañero pepper. Gently mix this up, and put the chicken pieces back in. They should be on top, yet slightly nestled into the sauce, not drowning in it. Cover and cook at a simmer for 30 to 45 minutes, or until the chicken falls off the bones. Serve this in shallow bowls, with a spoonful or two of sauce on the bottom, then the chicken, and a little extra chopped rosemary on top. You'll also want a nice hunk of a crusty baguette to soak up the extra sauce.

CRUNCHY GRATED CARROT SALAD WITH LIME
(CAROTTES RAPÉES)

X never kept much in his refrigerator—some milk for coffee, a few eggs, and usually hunks of Camembert and Roquefort cheeses stinking it up. And carrots. He always had this enormous container of pre-packaged shredded carrots.

Shredded carrots are a very French thing, and they are everywhere, at just about any grocer, *traiteur* (deli), and gas station convenience store along the autoroute, right there in the refrigerated section, next to the screw-top rosé and the single-serving containers of chocolate mousse. If there's a picnic, you can be certain that along with a quiche or two, someone's brought a big bowl of shredded carrots.

I didn't get it. They looked so uninspired. Too *orange.* But curiosity—and hunger—got the best of me one afternoon while X was at work. I carefully peeled back the plastic, and dug my fork in. They weren't soggy, as I'd assumed; they were crunchy, and the vinaigrette wasn't half-bad, either. Before I knew it, I'd eaten half of his of ready-to-eat carrots.

Which got me to thinking.

I wondered how much better they'd be if I gave the whole carrot thing a Cowgirl spin. As it turns out, way better. X hasn't eaten the store-bought carrots since.

CRUNCHY GRATED CARROT SALAD WITH LIME
(CAROTTES RAPÉES)

SERVES 6

about 1½ pounds/800 grams of carrots,
  peeled and shredded

a handful of fresh cilantro, chopped

the juice of 2 limes

2 to 3 tablespoons of sugar

a pinch of sea salt

a pinch of cumin

a pinch of cayenne pepper

Put your carrots in a super-big bowl and add everything else, tasting as you go. Serve right away.

MY BIG FAT
FRENCH SALAD

We met at a writer's workshop in Paris. Suzanne was a poet from Los Angeles who knitted words into powerful naked prose and read them out loud with unshakable confidence. She was tough and vulnerable, and I liked her instantly.

After the workshop, our small group hopped on a crowded city bus to go the Left Bank bookstore Shakespeare and Company, and Suzanne and I stood near the front, holding on to the dirty, smudged silver poles, already telling stories and giggling.

I'd only been in Paris for a few months, and I hadn't had a good laugh with a girlfriend since I'd arrived. Or with anyone. Even though Suzanne and I had just met, I already knew we were going to be friends.

The next week, we met for dinner—the first of many to follow—at Le Relais du Gascon in Montmartre, a place known for its enormous salads, about halfway up the steep hill to the iconic Sacré Coeur (the church with the Dairy Queen ice cream cone top).

Suzanne and I would laugh for hours over carafes of Gamay and the biggest salads I'd seen outside of Texas, mixing-bowl-size things, filled with heaps of lettuce, lots of *lardons* (Frenchy for small matchsticks of bacon), and melted goat cheese on toast, covered with a mountain of warm, garlicky roasted potatoes.

Hot potatoes on a salad? Inspired.

A great friendship grew out of those evenings, and I loved that particular Montmartre salad so much that I came up with my own, to eat at home.

MY BIG FAT FRENCH SALAD

½ pound/225 grams of red-skinned potatoes,
   cut into 2-inch/5 cm pieces

olive oil

sea salt and pepper

8 slices of bacon

6 slices from a baguette, toasted

about 6 tablespoons of fresh goat cheese

1 head of romaine lettuce, rinsed, dried,
   and sliced into 2-inch/5 cm strips

a handful of cherry tomatoes, halved

fresh herbs, such as chives, thyme, basil, and parsley

Champagne-Honey Vinaigrette (recipe follows)

1. Preheat your oven to 400°F/200°C. Put the potatoes on a parchment-lined cookie sheet, along with some olive oil, salt, and pepper, and toss this all together. Give the pan a shake so the potatoes aren't crowded, and slide them into the oven. They'll take about 30 to 45 minutes total, but after 15 or 20 minutes, the halfway mark, pull them out of the oven, and flip them over so both sides are evenly cooked.

2. Fry up the bacon. Once it's cooked and crispy, let it drain on paper towels. Don't forget to pour off the bacon grease into an old jam jar and keep it in the fridge; it'll make your cornbread (p.64 and p.210) fabulous.

3. Toast the baguette pieces, then put a heaping tablespoon of fresh goat cheese on each piece of toast and slide back into the oven for just a minute or two so the cheese can warm up.

4. To assemble your salads, divide the lettuce between two bowls, crumble the bacon over, add the warm potatoes, and arrange the cherry tomatoes and baguette pieces around the sides. Use your kitchen scissors to snip your fresh herbs on top, serve, and pass around the vinaigrette.

CHAMPAGNE-HONEY VINAIGRETTE

MAKES ABOUT 1 CUP/240 ML

1 shallot, finely chopped
¼ cup/60 ml of champagne vinegar
1 tablespoon of lemon juice + the zest of 1 lemon
2 teaspoons of Dijon mustard
1 tablespoon of honey
sea salt and pepper
¾ cup/180 ml of grapeseed oil

Combine everything but your oil along with a pinch of salt and pepper in a jam jar, and give it a shake so everything combines. Let this rest for 10 minutes or so. Add the grapeseed oil, and taste for seasonings.

> ★ **COWGIRL TIP:** When making vinaigrettes, let your own taste be your best guide. Add about half of the oil, shake it up, and add a bit more until you strike the right balance of oil and vinegar. I like my dressings slightly more vinegary, so I use less oil; you might like more oil.

CHAPTER 3

Souped Up

A little known fact about the French: They're crazy about soups. I've hardly had a meal in France, whether at the newest trendy bistro in Paris or dinner at an inn in the country that doesn't begin with something served in a bowl. There are *potages*, thick, stew-like soups; *veloutés* and *crèmes*, soups thickened with cream; clear bouillons and consommés; bisques made from shellfish and cream; *garbure*, a rustic soup made with ham and veggies; and, of course, there's just plain old soup. Or rather, *soupe*.

All of which makes me very happy, and very much like the French, at least in this one teensy way, because I, too, love soup. I've got at least four cookbooks devoted just to soups and a parrot green folder filled with soup recipes that I've collected over the years. If I can't think of what to make for dinner, I'll often pull together some kind of soup. Probably because I've spent so much of my life as a single girl and soups were easy to make and freeze, I still turn to soup as my default meal. Men have come and gone, but soups have never let me down.

In Texas, soups are traditionally cold-weather friends, but in France, soups are seasonless; they are a year-round, not just fall and winter, affair. I don't know why cold soups aren't eaten more in the summertime in Texas; you'd think they'd be the first thing people would think of when the thermostat gallops past the 100-degree mark. Paris, where air conditioning is still considered an unnecessary luxury and drinks come with just two ice cubes, taught me to turn to cold soups when the weather warms up.

Hot or cold, the proper way to eat soup is in a shallow bowl with a spoon that moves away from, not toward, your mouth. But I'll confess that I do not usually do this, and please do not mention this to my mother. I actually prefer my soup in big café au lait-size bowls, with an oversize spoon (I'll even use a coffee mug). I like to add crispy, crunchy, salty, or cheesy things to soup, to dress it up, to make it a little bit fancy. Soup deserves this extra attention. It has been there for me.

Soup Up Your Soup

As comforting as soup already is, it can still benefit from a little something extra. Smooth soups need crunch. Heavy soups and stews often need to be brightened up a bit. Monochromatic soups need a splash of color.

Besides, who wants to have a naked soup in the house?

1. Grate your favorite cheese—cheddar, Monterey Jack, Comté—and put it on top of your soup, or just crumble feta, queso fresco, or Roquefort. Shaved Parmesan or Pecorino-Romano is great, too.

2. Make soup croutons by tearing up stale bread and sprinkling the pieces with a bit of olive oil, sea salt, and pepper. Toss, put on a cookie sheet, and slide into a 400°F/200°C oven for 15 to 20 minutes.

3. Add a spoonful of Pico de Gallo (p. 319) to your soup.

4. Make a batch of caramelized onions (p.166) and add them to your soup.

5. Veggie soups love leftover bits of shredded chicken (p.89) or brisket (p. 155).

6. Toss some cooked grains into your soup (barley, rice, millet) to add texture. Quinoa is one of my favorites, too, and it's loaded with protein. Remember, it's always a ratio of 1:2/quinoa to water. Just boil your water, add the quinoa and cover your pot, reduce the heat, and set the timer for 10 minutes. Turn off the heat and let the quinoa rest for 10 minutes more. Fluff.

7. Nut oils, such as pistachio, walnut, and hazelnut, are great swirled into soups. So are herby and flavored oils, such as Lime-Cilantro Oil (p.135) and Basil Oil (p.97).

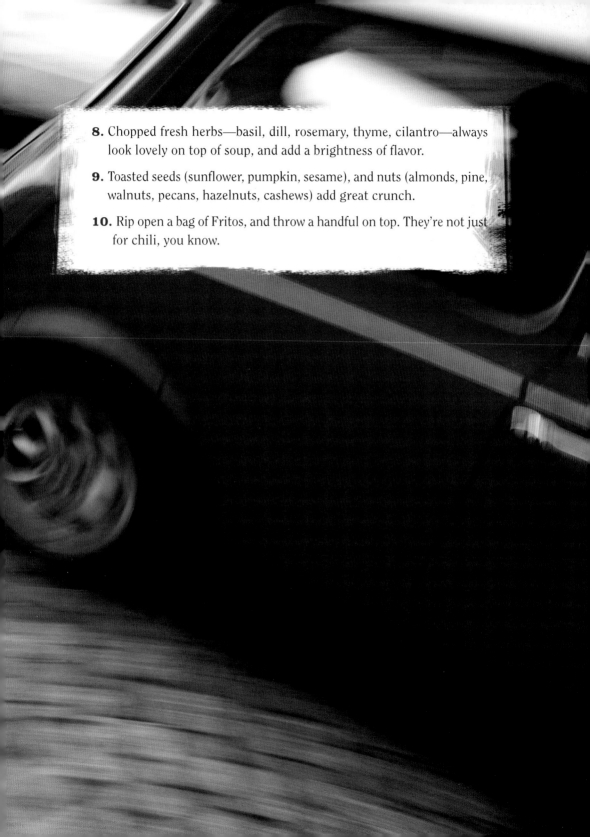

8. Chopped fresh herbs—basil, dill, rosemary, thyme, cilantro—always look lovely on top of soup, and add a brightness of flavor.

9. Toasted seeds (sunflower, pumpkin, sesame), and nuts (almonds, pine, walnuts, pecans, hazelnuts, cashews) add great crunch.

10. Rip open a bag of Fritos, and throw a handful on top. They're not just for chili, you know.

SMOKIN'
TORTILLA SOUP

This recipe is one of those things, like some wines and a few old boyfriends, that improve with age. Over time, I've added to, taken away, and swapped out different ingredients. What I've got now is what I believe to be the very best tortilla soup, ever—and believe me, I've tasted some tortilla soups in my day.

Some tortilla soups are clear and brothy, and on the thin side, with a few token tortilla strips thrown in at the last minute. This is not one of those. This is thickened with tortillas, first toasted till crisp, then puréed to give the soup some substance. If there's one thing I can't stand, it's a wimpy soup.

When I moved to Paris, I brought this recipe with me. Problem was, there weren't any corn tortillas around here. So I had to start making them (p.315) myself. Which you may do, too, if you so choose. I highly recommend it. Get out your tortilla press, call in those kids, and put them to work. These things don't have to be just so.

Great thing about this soup, besides the soup itself—which tastes like a big ol' bowl of Texas—is that it takes almost no time to put together. This is not one of those soups that taste better the next day. Well, I suppose it could be, but I always eat it right away until it's all gone and it just doesn't have time to sit around.

SMOKIN' TORTILLA SOUP

MAKES 4 SERVINGS

1 onion, cut into eight wedges

8 cloves of garlic, left in their skins

canola oil

6 Corn Tortillas (p.315), or you may use store-bought

1 (28-ounce/765 gram) can of whole tomatoes,
with their juices

1 canned chipotle in adobo

4 cups/1 liter of Save Your Scraps! Veggie Stock
(p.114) or Skin & Bones Chicken Stock (p.112)

sea salt and pepper

about 1 pound/500 grams of shredded cooked chicken*

Toasty Tortilla Strips (recipe follows)

1 avocado, chopped

a handful of fresh cilantro, chopped

1 lime, sliced into wedges

1. Preheat your broiler. Toss the onion pieces and the garlic cloves onto a foil-lined cookie sheet along with a little canola oil, and toss with your hands. Slide into the oven and broil until the onions char around the edges, about 10 to 15 minutes.

2. Put your tortillas directly on the rack directly beneath the onions and garlic and let them crisp at the same time. Just keep a close eye on this— it should all be ready about the same time.

3. When cool enough to handle, squeeze the garlic out of its skins and toss into a blender along with the charred onions, crispy tortillas (torn into pieces), tomatoes, chipotle, and veggie or chicken stock, and a big pinch of salt and pepper. Purée until smooth, then pour this into your soup pot. Turn the heat to medium, add the shredded chicken and give this a stir. Let this come to a boil, turn down the heat and simmer for another 15 or

20 minutes. Serve your soup in big bowls with a handful of Toasty Tortilla Strips, chunks of avocado, chopped cilantro, and lime wedges on the side.

* Use leftover Easy Roast Chicken (p.265), a store-bought rotisserie chicken, or poach your own. If poaching, here's all you do: Put your chicken thighs or breasts in a large stockpot, cover with water, and add 1 carrot, 1 celery stalk, 1 bay leaf, a teaspoon of dried oregano, 8 peppercorns, and a big pinch of sea salt. Turn the heat to high and bring to a boil, then reduce to a simmer for 20 to 30 minutes, or until the chicken falls off the bones or is tender. Let the chicken cool in the pot if you have time, then shred.

TOASTY TORTILLA STRIPS

8 Corn Tortillas
1 teaspoon of chili powder
$\frac{1}{2}$ teaspoon of sea salt
canola oil

1. Preheat your oven to 450°F/250°C.

2. Slice the corn tortillas into strips $\frac{1}{2}$ inch/12 mm wide and toss them in a bowl with the chile powder and sea salt. Add a little canola oil and mix it all up with your hands so the tortilla strips are evenly coated with the oil and seasonings.

3. Spread the strips out on a cookie sheet, and bake until they're nice and crispy, about 15 minutes. You'll need to watch them carefully, and flip them over halfway through cooking so they'll be crunchy all the way through.

★ **COWGIRL TIP:** I always make more Toasty Tortilla Strips than I need for this soup so I can use them for salads, too. Just throw them in a plastic bag and store in the fridge.

SWEET POTATO-
BUTTERMILK SOUP

As soon as I found sweet potatoes in France, I turned a corner. Saw brighter days ahead. My homesickness might never be completely cured, but it would certainly be less severe if sweet potatoes were in my life. Pricey as they were, I bought them by the kilo and made sweet potato anything I could think of—sweet potato fries, sweet potato pies, sweet potato biscuits (p.29), sweet potato hash browns.

I actually started this recipe in Texas one winter and finished it when I returned to France. It is not unlike a sweet potato pie. There is buttermilk instead of crème fraîche, because I was feeling particularly homesick, and liked the idea, anyway. And there are pecans, because they are a Texas thing; they're coated with a sugary-spicy combo that I adapted from a French recipe, but I got the idea from something similar a Texas friend brought me as a gift.

The tasty result is a soothing reminder that some cross-cultural combinations are deliciously effortless.

SWEET POTATO-BUTTERMILK SOUP

olive oil

1 shallot, finely chopped

1 clove of garlic, minced

1 teaspoon of peeled and finely chopped
fresh ginger

1 large sweet potato, peeled and chopped
into 2-inch/5 cm chunks

1 large carrot, peeled and chopped into
2-inch/5 cm pieces

3 cups/720 ml of Save Your Scraps! Veggie Stock
(p.114) or Skin & Bones Chicken Stock (p.112),
or you may use store-bought

½ cup/120 ml of buttermilk

sea salt

Happy Dance! Pecans (recipe follows)

1. Put your olive oil, shallot, garlic, and ginger in a large soup pot and turn
   the heat to medium-low. Cook for a few minutes, or until the shallots
   become translucent and, along with the garlic and ginger, give off a nice
   aroma—your nose will tell you when it's ready before your eyes will.

2. Toss in your sweet potato and carrots, add your veggie or chicken stock,
   and turn up the heat to medium-high. When it boils, reduce the heat to a
   simmer. Let this cook for about 20 more minutes, or until the sweet
   potato and carrots are soft. Carefully pour this into a blender, and add
   the buttermilk and a pinch of sea salt. Blend until it's smooth, then
   taste. Serve warm with a handful of roughly chopped Happy Dance!
   Pecans.

HAPPY DANCE! PECANS

MAKES 2 CUPS/ 230 GRAMS

2 cups/230 grams of pecans

4 tablespoons of butter

2 tablespoons of brown sugar

2 teaspoons of Worcestershire sauce

½ teaspoon of Tabasco sauce

2 teaspoons of smoked paprika or
  1 teaspoon of chipotle powder

¼ teaspoon of cayenne pepper

1 teaspoon of sea salt

¼ teaspoon of ground cinnamon

1. Line a baking sheet with parchment paper and set this aside.

2. Toast your pecans in a large nonstick skillet over medium-low heat. It won't take long – not even 10 minutes — so watch them carefully. Once they're nice and brown, add the rest of the ingredients and stir until the butter and sugar are melted, about 2 to 3 minutes. Transfer the pecans to the baking sheet, separate the nuts, and let them cool completely. Store your nuts in the fridge in an airtight plastic bag or in an old jam jar.

★ **COWGIRL TIP:** These will turn out better if you make them on a dry rather than humid day.

★ **DOUBLE-DUTY:** Well, you can just eat them by the handful (which you will), or toss these on top of salads, or make a whole bunch, put them in jars, and give them as gifts.

GAZPACHO

I realize gazpacho's a Spanish thing, but you'd never know that in France. Around the middle of May, cheery red and green containers of gazpacho appear on grocery store shelves, sandwiched between the endless white cartons of orange juice. One spring, to kick off cold soup season, the exuberant gazpacho-to-go people stationed themselves at the various entrances of the République metro station—one of the city's largest—and gave away samples of the blended tomato-and-veggie soup.

Or tried to. I watched with curiosity as Parisians reacted to this American-style promotion with suspicion. Things aren't free here. There's no try-before-you-buy policy—anywhere. It's buyer beware, not some silly notion about the customer always being right. Living in France, I learned pretty quickly that the customer is never right, and if you think you are and want to make your case, then good luck to you. If you get home from the store and realize that the sack of onions you just bought is rotten, well, congratulations, you're now the proud owner of a sack of bad onions. Sure, you can try to take them back and you can try to find a manager who may or may not be there, because it is very likely that he: a) is on a cigarette break; b) has already gone home, having met his government-mandated, 35-hour per week requirement; or c) is on vacation. If he is there (and chances are good that it will be a he), go ahead and try to explain—*en français, s'il vous plaît*—that the onions are bad and you would like your money back. Or, just do what I do, and toss the onions into *la poubelle* and make something else instead.

And resolve to shop the twice-weekly markets. It isn't always convenient, but the produce is always better than what you'll find in the grocery stores, including all the ingredients for gazpacho.

GAZPACHO

2 pounds/1 kilo of tomatoes

½ of an onion, roughly chopped

1 red bell pepper, roughly chopped

1 green bell pepper, roughly chopped

1 cucumber, peeled and seeded, plus 1 small
    cucumber, diced, for serving (about 1 cup)

1 garlic clove, minced

2 tablespoons of red wine vinegar

¼ cup of olive oil

sea salt and pepper

1 avocado, diced

2 eggs, hardboiled and roughly chopped

a handful of tortilla strips (p.89)

1. With a serrated knife, make an X on the bottoms of your tomatoes, just
slicing through the skin. Put a pot of water on to boil, and when it's bubbling, add your tomatoes and set the timer for 30 seconds—we're just
blanching them, not cooking them. Remove the tomatoes and peel off
the skins. Now, cut them in half and squeeze out the seeds.

2. That was the hard part. Now you can just toss the tomatoes, onion, red
and green peppers, the peeled, seeded cucumber, garlic, red wine vinegar, olive oil, and a big pinch of salt and pepper into your blender and
pulse until the mixture is coarse (this is a rustic dish and you don't want
it to be too smooth). Taste for seasonings and refrigerate for 2 to 3 hours.
Serve this in shallow bowls and pass around the chopped avocado, eggs,
the diced cucumber, and tortilla strips.

> ★ **COWGIRL TIP:** Make gazpacho early in the day and let it rest.
> It'll be better that way.

BROCCOLI-BASIL SOUP

I think that everyone should love broccoli, and I never understand it when people don't. Even though X says he doesn't like broccoli, I'm convinced that if I just keep giving it to him in disguise, like you would with a kid, he'll come around. And I have good reason to believe this: He'll eat broccoli if it's stir-fried, and he doesn't mind it in the Roasted Broccoli-Red Bell Pepper Tart (p.182). So I figured that he'd like it in this soup, too, because you don't actually *see* the broccoli.

I also know that if I throw in a bit of cheese and bread to distract him (as I've done here with these goat cheese croutons), he'll be finishing up the first bowl and asking for more before he figures out what he's just eaten. Which is exactly what happened when I first made this.

Call me sneaky, but it's just a little trick that I learned from my mom, who used to hide carrots—which I did not like as a child—in her meaty spaghetti sauce and in her meatloaf, too.

Of course I ended up loving carrots.

I figure this broccoli thing with X is just a matter of time.

BROCCOLI-BASIL SOUP WITH GOAT CHEESE TOASTS

olive oil

1 shallot, finely chopped

1 large head of broccoli, florets removed and the stalk, peeled then chopped into 1-inch/2.5 cm pieces

4 cups/1 liter of Save Your Scraps! Veggie Stock (p.114) or Skin & Bones Chicken Stock (p.112), or you may use store-bought

a handful of fresh basil leaves

sea salt and pepper

½ of a baguette, thinly sliced and toasted

5 ounces/150 grams of fresh goat cheese

Basil Oil (recipe follows)

1. Put a little olive oil in your stockpot and add the shallots. Turn the heat to medium-low and let the shallots cook for a few minutes, just until they're translucent. Add your broccoli and vegetable stock. Put the lid on, and bring this to a boil over medium heat.

2. Once it boils, turn the heat down and simmer until the broccoli stems are soft—this'll only take about 15 to 20 minutes. Carefully pour your soup into a blender—you'll probably need to work in batches so you don't spray yourself with hot soup—then add the basil and a big pinch of sea salt and pepper. (Blend some of the basil, salt, and pepper with each batch of soup if working in batches.) Purée until smooth and taste for seasonings. Serve warm with baguette toasts spread with goat cheese, and a swirl of Basil Oil.

> ★ **DOUBLE-DUTY:** This soup will also work as a pasta sauce. Just heat up your favorite chunky pasta—I love penne—and toss with a couple of spoonfuls of Super-Quick Homemade Ricotta (p.173, a bit more torn basil, and the Basil Oil.

BASIL OIL
MAKES ABOUT ½ CUP/120 ML

15 large fresh basil leaves
1 tablespoon of finely chopped shallot
½ cup /120 ml of olive oil
¼ teaspoon of lime or lemon zest
a pinch of sea salt and pepper

Put all of the ingredients in a small food processor and pulse until blended. Pour into an old jam jar and refrigerate for a half-hour, at least, before using. This'll keep for a few days in the fridge.

> ★ **COWGIRL TIP:** Fresh basil will keep for at least a week if you trim the stems and stuff it into a vase with fresh water, changing it every day or two, and trimming the ends each time.

MINTY
CANTALOUPE SOUP

By Texas standards, summers in Paris aren't really that hot, but if you don't have air conditioning in your teensy apartment, then it's a whole different story, especially when you consider the impact of the city itself—an island of concrete that radiates warmth like the floor heater at my grandmother's house.

Smart people leave the city and go to their country homes for a month or two, where cool breezes blow from the mountains, or head straight to the sea. But since I haven't yet found the perfect Normandy château or seaside flat on the Île de Ré, I've come up with a few summer survival techniques in the meantime.

Fans on four-foot-high stands in each room of our tiny apartment push the warm air around nonstop, which means that there's a constant roar over which the volume of everything from conversations to the television must be increased. I drink lots of iced coffee, even though I'm constantly reminded by X that I should drink water instead. Coffee *is* water, I tell him. Water that's been enhanced and improved. I also eat lighter—and later, too—since the summer sun doesn't set until well past 10 p.m.

And I make lots of cold soups.

Like this one. And yes, I know it may sound weird to put Roquefort on top of a cold melon soup, but that's exactly what makes this wonderful.

MINTY
CANTALOUPE SOUP

MAKES 4 SERVINGS

2 ripe cantaloupes, peeled, seeded,
   and cut into chunks

the juice of 1 lemon

6 large fresh basil leaves,
   plus a bit more for serving

8 fresh mint leaves,
   plus a bit more for serving

a pinch of sea salt

about 1 ounce/30 grams of crumbled
   Roquefort cheese

about 1 ounce/30 grams of toasted
   almond slivers

1. Put your cantaloupe pieces in your blender along with the lemon juice, basil, mint, and salt, and purée until it's very smooth. Chill down in the fridge for at least 3 hours before serving.

2. Pour the soup into bowls and garnish with a bit of Roquefort, toasted almonds, and some torn basil and mint leaves.

MINESTRONE

One chilly October, I was in Florence having lunch with a friend of mine at a trattoria not far from the Arno River. We ordered the daily soup, *ribollita*, which is basically minestrone's last gasp—after a day or two, what's left is put in a pot along with whatever stale bread's still hanging around, and you get a "boiled again" soup that's thick and bready. It was—and remains—the perfect thing for a chilly autumn day.

Like so many Florentine dishes, this rustic soup won me over. Served with a swirl of fruity local olive oil and a couple of glasses of red wine, the *ribollita* made for a lunch I've never forgotten. I can still remember how it warmed me right down to my bones.

There are vegetable soups, and then there's minestrone, the vegetable soup that tastes like a lazy afternoon in Florence. Paris isn't Florence, but when it's cold and damp in France and I hear it's 80 or 90 degrees back in Texas, there's nothing like a Florentine minestrone. Served as is or puréed till it's creamy or bolstered with bread and made into *ribollita*, it's as good one way as the next. And when it's all gone, I'm usually thinking about when I'm going to make it again.

MINESTRONE

olive oil

2 leeks, sliced (white parts only)

2 cloves of garlic, minced

a few fresh basil leaves

3 carrots, peeled and chopped

2 celery stalks, chopped

2 zucchini (one green and one yellow), chopped

4 new potatoes, chopped into 2-inch/5 cm pieces

1 (28-ounce/765 gram can) of diced
    tomatoes with their juices

4 cups/1 liter of Skin & Bones Chicken
    Stock (p.112), or you may use store-bought

1 (6-ounce/170 gram can) of tomato paste

3 bay leaves

1 teaspoon of dried thyme

½ teaspoon of red pepper flakes

the rind of 1 piece of Parmesan cheese

sea salt and pepper

1 (14.5-ounce/395 gram can) of cannellini
    beans, drained and rinsed

a handful of shredded Chinese cabbage
    (it's also called Napa cabbage)

a handful of fresh spinach

1. Drizzle some olive oil into your biggest stockpot and add the leeks, garlic, and basil. Turn the heat to medium-low and let this cook, stirring
   every now and then, until the leeks begin to soften.

2. Add the carrots and let them cook for a few minutes, then add your celery, and let this cook for a couple of minutes, too. After the celery and carrots have softened slightly, now you can toss in almost everything else—the zucchini, potatoes, diced tomatoes, chicken stock, tomato paste, bay leaves, thyme, red pepper flakes, and the Parmesan cheese rind—this is the key to the soup's great flavor. Season with a big pinch of sea salt and pepper, cover loosely, and let this cook on low heat for about 2 hours, or until the potatoes are cooked. Then add the cannellini beans, and let them warm through for about 10 minutes.

3. Taste again for seasonings, then right before serving, add the cabbage and spinach—it won't take but a minute or two to cook. Garnish your soup with a swirl of Basil Oil (p.97).

> ★ **GREAT WITH:** Cheesy Rosemary-Olive Flatbread (p.50).

ZUCCHINI-
CILANTRO SOUP

When I was still living in Dallas and I'd come to Paris to visit X, while he was off at work, instead of studying French and trying to sort out the difference between the plus-que-parfait and the passé composé tenses, I'd walk down the street to The Village Voice Bookshop and thumb through the English-language books. I always loved seeing the owner Odile Hillier's picks, which she'd stack on a large wooden table near the front window, with handwritten cards folded over the covers of her favorites, explaining why each book was chosen. I loved that she actually took the time to read the books she sold, and I always found something I needed to buy that I'd not yet heard of.

I tried to time my book shopping right before lunch, so afterward I could take my new book to the restaurant across the street that served a half dozen or so fresh soups each day.

I got the zucchini soup right off the bat because I loved its pretty green color and I'd never tasted zucchini soup before. It was creamy, zucchini-y, and so simple. Nothing else, just that.

Back in Dallas, I started making my own, but without cream, because I didn't think that it needed it, and with lots of cilantro. This soup's great on its own, just as it is, with a squeeze of lime—but I like it even more with DQ-style mix-ins. Like a Blizzard on a road trip, it's just more fun that way.

ZUCCHINI-CILANTRO SOUP

MAKES 4 TO 6 SERVINGS

olive oil

1 shallot, finely chopped

1 potato, peeled and cubed

4 large zucchini (about 2 pounds/1 kilo), cut into fat slices, and 1 medium zucchini, cut into fat sticks about 2 inches/5 cm long (see Cowgirl Tip)

2 cups/480 ml of Save Your Scraps! Veggie Stock (p.114) or Skin & Bones Chicken Stock (p.112), or you may use store-bought

sea salt and pepper

1 bunch of cilantro with stems

6 Oven-Roasted Tomatoes (p.197), chopped

4 to 6 tablespoons of fresh goat cheese

a handful of toasted slivered almonds

1. Pour a little bit of olive oil into a your soup pot, toss in the minced shallots, and turn the heat to medium-low. Cook for a few minutes, just until the shallots become translucent. Add your potatoes, 2 cups/480 ml of water, and put the lid on. Cook until the potatoes begin to soften, about 10 minutes. Now, toss in your zucchini slices, the 2 cups/480 ml of vegetable or chicken stock, a good pinch of salt and pepper, and turn the heat to low. Keep your pot covered, and let this go until the zucchini softens, not more than 10 to 15 minutes.

2. While the soup's cooking, roast your zucchini sticks. Preheat the oven to broil. Put the zucchini pieces onto a parchment-lined cookie sheet and toss with a bit more olive oil. Sprinkle with salt and pepper, and slide this into the oven for 10 to 15 minutes, making sure to flip the zucchini pieces over about halfway through.

3. Add the cilantro to the soup pot, and either purée the soup with your hand blender, or if you want it super-smooth like I do, use your blender. Taste for seasonings, and serve warm in bowls with a few pieces of roasted zucchini, and about a tablespoon of each: chopped oven-roasted tomato, fresh goat cheese, and roasted slivered almonds.

> ★ **COWGIRL TIP:** To make zucchini sticks, simply cut off the top and bottom of your zucchini, then slice it into 2-inch/5 cm chunks. Now cut each one of these in half, making two fat half-moons. Put each one on the cutting board, flat-side down, and slice your zucchini into small "sticks."

30-MINUTE TOMATO SOUP *with* GRILLED CHEESE CROUTONS

OR, "HOW I OUTSMART TOMATOES," PART I

Ages ago, I used to make a tomato soup entirely with slow-roasted tomatoes. It was not a 30-minute soup. It was a two-day soup. Pounds of tomatoes first had to be bought and roasted; the soup I made after that. It was a great soup. It still is.

I don't know about you, but to me, tomato soup's one of those things, like grilled cheese sandwiches, that I want right away, and I usually want them together. Waiting is not an option.

With a craving for tomato soup one fall afternoon, I opened my kitchen cabinet and saw a jar of sundried tomatoes just sitting there on the shelf, and I knew, I just knew, that this was my answer, to an almost-instant tomato soup.

Made with sundried and canned tomatoes, this soup tasted so much like one I used to make with slow-roasted tomatoes that I scrapped that recipe and kept on making this one. Now I save my slow-roasted tomatoes for other things (Winter BLT Tartines, p.196; Roasted Ratatouille, p.231), and I can have homemade tomato soup any old time I want it.

30-MINUTE
TOMATO SOUP WITH
GRILLED CHEESE CROUTONS

MAKES 4 SERVINGS

olive oil

2 cloves of garlic, minced

1 (8-ounce/227 gram) jar of sundried tomatoes in oil, drained (be sure to save the oil in the fridge for vinaigrettes)

1 (28-ounce/765 gram) can of crushed tomatoes

2 cups /½ liter of Save Your Scraps! Veggie Stock (p.114) or Skin & Bones Chicken Stock (p.112)

1 cup/240 ml of water

2 tablespoons of butter, melted

4 thin slices of brioche (my favorite) or white sandwich bread

about 4 tablespoons of grated cheddar cheese

a handful of fresh thyme, leaves removed

1. Put some olive oil in your stockpot along with the minced garlic and turn the heat to medium-low. When you begin to smell the garlic—and you will after just a minute or two—add the sundried tomatoes, crushed tomatoes, stock, and water. Bring this to a boil over medium heat, then reduce heat to a simmer and let it cook for 30 minutes.

2. While the soup's cooking, make your grilled cheese croutons: put 1 to 2 tablespoons of cheese on each slice of bread (this will depend on how big your bread slices are), sprinkle over a few fresh thyme leaves, and top with the remaining 2 pieces of bread. Brush one side of each sandwich with the melted butter, and put this side down onto a hot skillet over medium-low heat. Let this cook until brown and crispy, brushing the tops of the sandwiches with the rest of the melted butter. Flip the sandwiches over and cook the other side until brown and crispy. When the

sandwiches are done, cut them diagonally into fourths, then eighths, and finally, 16ths—now you've got lots of little triangles of grilled cheese sandwich croutons.

3. Purée your soup with a hand blender (or use your blender if you want it super-smooth), divide among serving bowls, and toss a few grilled cheese croutons on top, along with some fresh thyme.

> ★ **COWGIRL TIP**: Melting your butter, then brushing it onto your bread when making any sort of grilled sandwich, ensures that the browning will be even, and you won't have those big "butter spots."

SKIN & BONES CHICKEN STOCK

I love the idea of always making chicken stock with a whole chicken, but more often than not, I've got a freezer full of leftover chicken carcasses and I'm needing to make space for something else, like ice cream, right away. So I make stock, and as with my veggie scraps stock (p.113), I get the added satisfaction of feeling super-thrifty. No matter how awful the dollar-to-euro exchange rate is, if I've made my own stock I can end the day feeling like I'm a little bit ahead.

It's something my mom always did, and because of her, I've never been able to toss a perfectly good chicken carcass in the trash. Not with all of those still-tasty bits of meat clinging to the bones.

If you've never made stock before, fear not. It pretty much makes itself. You just need to peek into the pot every now and then to make sure it's bubbling slowly, blurp-blurp-blurp, just as it should.

SKIN & BONES
CHICKEN STOCK

MAKES ABOUT 4 QUARTS/4 LITERS

1 to 2 chicken carcasses

5 quarts/5 liters of water

1 onion, quartered

1 carrot, peeled and halved

1 celery stalk, halved

about 20 peppercorns

3 bay leaves

5 sprigs of fresh thyme

5 sprigs of fresh parsley

sea salt

1. Get out your biggest stockpot and throw in your chicken carcasses. Cover with 5 quarts/5 liters of water and turn the heat on high. Once this boils, carefully skim off the foam (not the fat, which will give the stock great flavor).

2. Add the onion, carrot, celery, peppercorns, bay leaves, thyme, and parsley (which you can tie together with a string if you want to be neat—I usually just throw it all in), and a big pinch of salt. Loosely cover, turn the heat down to a simmer, and let this cook for 5 hours. Towards the end, taste, and if you need to add a bit more salt, this is the time (or you may skip the salt altogether). Strain through a piece of cheesecloth pressed into a colander, and let cool.

SAVE YOUR SCRAPS!
VEGGIE STOCK

One afternoon, I read a blog post by Theresa Murphy, who also lives in Paris and teaches classes on organic vegetarian cuisine, about what you can do with the odd bits and pieces of vegetables that you normally toss right into the garbage or compost—onion skins, the tops of bell peppers, carrot peels, the leafy tops of celery, things like that.

Vegetable stock, she said. We should be saving these scraps instead of throwing them away.

Well, of course. I couldn't believe I hadn't thought of it before. I'd always saved my chicken carcasses for chicken stock (p.112), and my shrimp shells for fish stock (p.249) but I'd never thought of making vegetable stock from scraps.

I hated thinking about all of the scraps I'd tossed out in my lifetime. Enough to stretch from France to Texas and back a few times, I imagined.

Right then, I vowed to save my scraps, always make veggie stock, and change my wasteful ways.

SAVE YOUR SCRAPS!
VEGGIE STOCK

MAKES ABOUT 4 QUARTS/4 LITERS

1 (1 quart/1 liter) plastic bag filled
   with scraps (carrot peelings, onion skin, celery leaves,
   zucchini ends, or whatever you've collected)

3 bay leaves

20 peppercorns

a few sprigs of fresh herbs, such as
   thyme, basil, and parsley

5 quarts/5 liters of water

a big pinch of sea salt

Put everything in a large stockpot and bring this to a boil. Cover, turn the heat down to a simmer, and cook for 4 hours. Taste, and add more salt if needed (or you may simply leave out the salt if you'd rather). Strain the stock through a piece of cheesecloth placed over a colander on top of a large bowl. Let your stock cool completely and either use right away or freeze.

> ★ **COWGIRL TIP:** I like to freeze my stock in 2 cup/½ liter and 4 cup/1 liter containers, since those are the sizes that I use the most when making soups.

CHAPTER 4

Greens

The wooing actually began with the simplest of salads—endive stuffed with Roquefort. Then he moved on to something bigger and more impressive, served one summer on a balcony overlooking the Atlantic in Biarritz. Hearts of palm, mushrooms, ham, hard-boiled eggs, summer tomatoes, cucumbers. Cue the blazing sunset. I was toast.

Since then, I've taken over the salad-making in our household, and I've learned that salads—even a few leaves of lettuce tossed with some fresh herbs —are as much a part of an everyday French dinner as wine and a baguette.

I've never seen so many kinds of lettuce. There are enormous ruffled heads in purple or green; torpedo-shaped endive, the perennial French favorite; *sucrines,* which look like baby romaine; curly and slightly bitter *frisée;* watercress; *mâche;* radicchio; and mesclun, a mix of them all.

Eating lots of salads is nothing new for me. Whether I'm alone or having a group over for dinner, I love the idea of a big bowl of something fluffy and green that's passed around the table. Like the French, I eat salads both at the beginning and at the end of a meal, or along with—and sometimes right on top of—whatever I'm eating. I've always put arugula on homemade pizza, just like they do in Italy, and now I heap it right onto slices of tarts.

Salads can be anything you want them to be: big productions with lots of different textures and colors, tossed with an herby vinaigrette, a simple lettuce-lemon-oil-salt-and-pepper number, or anything in between. Salads welcome spontaneity. They invite play. There are very few rules with salads. You start with a bowl or a big plate and open the fridge. There's a salad lurking in there somewhere.

Even though the word for salad in French is *salade,* the similarities stop there. A French *salade* is not an American salad and never will be.

Consider:

A *salade* in France doesn't always mean salad; a *salade* can also be just veggies, or noodles, or noodles and veggies, or beans, or any combination of the above. Fruit. Bread. Fish. Chicken. Pork. You get the idea.

There are no salad bars here. If you order a salad—anywhere—you will never be offered a choice of dressings and it will never come on the side. The salad will be dressed for you, and lightly, with a vinaigrette, and while there may be thick, greasy bacon bits (*lardons*), there will not be croutons.

If you order an omelette or a croque monsieur at a brasserie, even in a small country town, it will always come with a salad on the side. Not *frites,* not potato chips. A salad.

Along with melted goat cheese, canned corn is a popular brasserie salad topping; I've seen corn served no other way than sprinkled on top of lettuce, which may be why it only comes in tiny cans.

Lettuce is not torn into bite-size pieces, and the leaves are never sliced before eaten; rather, salads are eaten by patiently folding the lettuce leaves as many times as it takes with your knife and fork to create a manageable mouthful.

SUNDAY TUNA SALAD

If you live in Paris and you've not gotten up early on Sunday morning and gone either to the market or to one of the few grocery stores that are open until 1 p.m., then you're out of luck.

This is merely a scheduling issue, you're probably thinking. Who can't rearrange their Sunday morning to get to the store?

Well, I can't. Or don't, usually. My Sundays go like this: I wake up, I drink a whole bunch of coffee, and I read *The New York Times* online. Leisurely. I might walk Rose. I might go to a late yoga class. When I'm finished with all of this, it's usually around 1 p.m., exactly when the markets and grocery stores close.

I don't know how the French got this one so wrong. They work for just thirty-five hours a week. They take two-hour lunches. It's not uncommon to have a 10:30 p.m. dinner reservation on a Saturday night, and to finish well past 1 a.m.

Yet they wake up early on a Sunday morning to go *grocery shopping?*

I've learned that a 7 p.m. cocktail party never starts before 8:30 p.m., and I'm no longer surprised when I go to the butcher's at 1:45 and he asks if I can come back after 4, because it is nearly time for him to break for lunch. Transportation strikes no longer phase me, sketchy Internet service is a given, and handymen who need three to four weeks' notice and then forget to show up are the rule, not the exception.

But this Sunday morning grocery shopping business I just can't get used to.

This is what I made one Sunday night when I had very little in the fridge, even less in the cabinet, and half of a stale baguette from the night before. I liked it so much that now I'll go shopping just to buy things to make this salad. But of course, never on a Sunday.

SUNDAY TUNA SALAD

MAKES 2 DINNER-SIZE
OR 4 FIRST-COURSE SALADS

a big handful of cherry tomatoes, halved

1 (6-ounce/160 gram)* can of tuna packed
   in olive oil, drained

a handful of kalamata olives, split in half
   and pits removed

2 tablespoons of capers, drained and rinsed

about ⅔ of a day-old baguette,
   cut into cubes (about 4 cups)

1 clove of garlic, minced

olive oil

sea salt and pepper

2 eggs

a big handful of arugula

a small handful of fresh basil, roughly torn

Basil Oil (p.97)

1. Preheat your oven to 450°F/230°C. Throw the halved tomatoes, tuna, capers, and kalamata olives in a big salad bowl.

2. Tear the baguette into 1-inch/2.5 cm pieces (or thereabouts—you can slice them if you want them to be the same size, but I like to just tear it up, because it's easier), and toss them onto a parchment-lined cookie sheet, along with the garlic. Drizzle a little olive oil on the croutons and garlic and toss it all around with your hands to make sure all of the croutons are covered in oil and the garlic is evenly distributed. Bake for 15 to 20 minutes, keeping a close eye on the little croutons, and flipping them over if needed, until they're crispy all the way through.

3. Put the eggs in a small saucepan, cover with cold water, add a pinch of salt, and bring to a boil. When the water boils, turn the heat down to a

simmer and set the timer for 10 minutes. When the buzzer goes off, put the saucepan in the sink, run cold water over it, and take out your eggs. Peel and roughly chop them up.

4. When you're ready to eat, add the chopped eggs to the big bowl, along with the cooled croutons, arugula, and basil. Add a couple of tablespoons of the basil oil on top, toss, and taste for seasonings.

* This is the largest can of tuna in oil in France, which is what I use, but if you'd like more tuna in your salad, or if the tuna where you live comes in larger cans, just add more.

★ **ADVANCE PLANNING:** You can make the croutons and boiled eggs ahead of time.

★ **SWAP IT:** Use leftover salmon instead of tuna.

IT'S THE
BERRIES SALAD

Fruit salads at our house were always a special affair. Strawberries came from my grandparents' strawberry patch at their farm outside of Ardmore, Oklahoma. We'd pick them ourselves, spending weekend afternoons on our knees, filling up the previous year's saved milk cartons with the fat, juicy berries. Melons were always balled, never simply sliced into chunks (it was years before I knew you could eat them any other way). And if the occasion was grand enough, we'd have an oniony-sweet poppy seed dressing served on the side in a small crystal pitcher made from a recipe that my grandmother handed down to my mom.

While I love each fruit and berry on its own—I routinely eat a container of raspberries on the walk home from the market, popping them into my mouth like M&Ms—I also like to mix them together, just like my mom did, then dress them with something that's a little bit savory, both to offset and intensify their natural sweetness.

IT'S THE BERRIES SALAD

MAKES 4 SERVINGS

2 big handfuls of arugula

12 ounces/340 grams of strawberries,
  hulled and halved

8 ounces/225 grams of raspberries

2 oranges, supremed (see Cowgirl Tip)

Orange Vinaigrette (recipe follows)

Put your arugula in a bowl and add the strawberries, raspberries, and orange pieces. Drizzle with Orange Vinaigrette, and gently toss. Serve immediately.

ORANGE VINAIGRETTE

MAKES ABOUT 1/3 CUP/75 ML

1 small shallot, finely chopped (about 1 tablespoon)

the juice of 1 orange

sea salt and pepper

about ¼ cup/60 ml of grapeseed oil

Put your chopped shallot, orange juice, and a big pinch of sea salt and pepper in a jam jar and shake it up. Let it rest for about 10 minutes, add the oil, and shake again. Taste for seasonings.

> ★ **COWGIRL TIP:** Supreming sounds hard, but it's really easy. Here's all you do: Using a sharp paring knife, slice off your orange's thick skin, making sure to get the white membrane, too. Simply slice between the membranes (which act like walls between the segments), and you'll get perfect slices— and no pith.

LES HALLES
SPINACH SALAD

I never thought about putting a poached egg on top of a salad when I lived in Dallas; in fact, I never gave eggs that much thought at all. I made frittatas occasionally, and scrambled eggs for breakfast tacos, but that's as far as eggs and I went.

Then I moved to Paris, and it was eggs, eggs, eggs, all over the place. Eggs on pizzas. Eggs mixed into raw ground beef and served as *steak tartare*. Eggs cooked in red wine and onions in cute little *cocottes* and served as a first course called *oeufs en meurette*. Eggs on top of inside-out ham sandwiches called croque madame. And everywhere I went, pâtisserie and boulangerie cases were filled with eggy tarts, quiches, flans, and crèmes brûlées.

Grocery stores routinely devote a number of shelves (always unrefrigerated) to eggs, labeled *moyen* (medium), *gros* (large), and *matins* ("mornings"). French laws require each egg to be stamped with a number in red ink, which corresponds to the sort of life the hen has enjoyed. Number-three eggs are laid by hens in crowded, industrial chicken prisons, which I avoid. Partially free-range are twos, and free-range are stamped with a number one. An egg stamped with a zero is considered the top; it's both organic and free-range.

With their tangerine-orange yolks, French eggs are creamy and rich. Intensely eggy. Fried, poached, scrambled, served simply on toast or as the centerpiece of a spinach salad, they're so good they've become my default meal when I don't have anything else planned.

I first ordered this spinach and egg salad at a little bistro near Les Halles, the area that was the city's central marketplace from medieval times until the 1970s, and quickly adapted it. I'll often make it with the super-fresh eggs I get from a friend who keeps chickens and call it dinner.

LES HALLES SPINACH SALAD

MAKES 2 DINNER-SIZE SALADS

2 big handfuls (about 5 ounces/
    150 grams) of baby spinach
8 pieces of thinly sliced prosciutto
a small wedge of Parmesan cheese
2 eggs
E-Z French Vinaigrette (recipe follows)
sea salt and pepper

1. Divide the spinach between two big plates, heaping it up in the middle
   like a big spinach mountain. Put 4 pieces of the prosciutto on each salad,
   and with your vegetable peeler, make curls of Parmesan on top. Now, go
   poach your eggs.

2. Put about 4 inches/10 cm of water in a deep skillet or saucepan along
   with a big pinch of salt, and turn the heat on high. When the water boils,
   turn it down to a simmer. Crack your eggs one at a time into a small glass
   bowl and ever so gently pour the egg from the bowl into the barely bubbling water. Set your timer for 2 minutes. With a slotted spoon, remove
   each egg and put the egg and spoon on a paper towel to absorb the moisture for a few seconds before carefully putting it on top of the spinach.
   Pass the vinaigrette and salt and pepper. Stab that yolk.

E-Z FRENCH VINAIGRETTE

MAKES ¾ CUP/180 ML

¼ cup/60 ml of sherry vinegar
1 shallot, finely chopped
1 teaspoon of Dijon mustard
sea salt and pepper
1 teaspoon of chopped fresh herbs
    (basil, thyme, chives)
½ cup/120 ml of olive oil

Put your sherry vinegar, minced shallot, mustard, a big pinch of salt and pepper and herbs in a jam jar, and shake, shake, shake. Let this rest for about 10 minutes—this softens the intensity of the shallot's flavor and allows the salt to dissolve. Now, add your olive oil, and shake again. Taste for seasonings.

★ **COWGIRL TIP:** This is the classic French vinaigrette, good for salads and over veggies, too. Highlight this one; you'll use it often.

END OF SUMMER
SALAD

I didn't want to call this salad "End of Summer Salad." I didn't want summer to end. But I knew, I just knew, sort of like an impending breakup, it was almost over. I didn't need to say it out loud. It was goodbye to the last good tomatoes and the few remaining peaches of the season.

I shouldn't get attached to seasons, and I certainly shouldn't be so silly about fruit and vegetables. I know this. They have seasons. They are here, and then they are gone. This is how it goes.

I can sense the clock ticking the moment they arrive, and I know not just the sellers who sell the ever-changing fruits and vegetables at the weekly markets but also exactly where they put them in their stands, whether it's on the left or the right, or perhaps on the very end, far on the corner. I know where to look and what to look for, and when I don't see it, I notice. I ask. How much longer will we have tomatoes, I'll say, afraid of hearing the answer, *Ils sont finis*.

Finished. Over. Gone.

But unlike a real breakup, they won't be gone forever. They'll be back next year, and they'll bring the summer with them.

END OF SUMMER SALAD

1 avocado

2 medium tomatoes

2 medium peaches

4.5 ounces/125 grams of fresh goat cheese

a handful of fresh basil, roughly torn

a handful of toasted almonds

Basil Pesto Vinaigrette (recipe follows)

sea salt and pepper

Chop up your avocado, tomatoes, and peaches into pieces roughly the same size and put them in a medium bowl. Add some of the Basil Pesto Vinaigrette and gently toss. Taste for seasonings, add the fresh goat cheese, toasted almonds, and torn pieces of basil—looks so pretty when you put it on the table—then toss again at tableside, like you're a waiter at a fancy restaurant. Serve immediately

BASIL PESTO VINAIGRETTE
MAKES ABOUT ½ CUP/120 ML

1 shallot, finely chopped

3 tablespoons of freshly squeezed lemon juice

2 teaspoons of Dijon mustard

1 big tablespoon of Basil Pesto (p.41), or you may use
  store-bought

sea salt and pepper

6 tablespoons of grapeseed oil

Put your shallots, lemon juice, Dijon mustard, Basil Pesto and a pinch of salt and pepper in a jam jar and give it a good shake. Let it rest for about 10 minutes; add the oil and shake again. Taste for seasonings.

BEETS and CLEMENTINES SALAD

Winters in Paris are brutal. No one tells you that. But they are.

I arrived in February, freezing, and spent the next few months (it was a very cold spring, too) feeling like I'd made a huge mistake. I missed the sun. I longed for warmth. Ugg boots seemed to be the only sensible choice when it came to footwear. Everywhere I went, I wore a down coat that nearly covered my ankles. It looked like a sleeping bag. I was still cold.

Over the next year or two, I not only got used to the long winters, I actually started to look forward to them. I embraced the gray. I welcomed the rain. And the snow—oh how beautiful Paris looks when it's covered in snow! I amassed an impressive collection of scarves, boots, sweaters, wool coats (no more down), and hats, so no matter how cold it got, I was prepared.

Nevertheless, there's a point when enough is enough. When you know that spring is coming, but it still seems so far away.

This is where this salad comes in. Beets, one of the season's finest offerings, and sunshiny clementines team up to let winter know that its time is almost up, and that brighter days are ahead.

BEETS AND
CLEMENTINES SALAD

MAKES 4 SERVINGS

3 medium beets

5 clementines (Mandarin oranges), peeled

E-Z French Vinaigrette (p.126)

a small chunk (about 2 ounces/55 grams)
  of crumbled feta

a small handful of fresh dill, chopped

1. Preheat your oven to 400°F/200°C.

2. Trim the ends off the beets, give them a good rinse and dry, and wrap
them up with heavy-duty foil (or about 10 pieces of foil if you live in
France, where the foil is like tissue paper). Put your beets on a cookie
sheet and slide them into the oven to bake for an hour, depending on the
size of your beets. To check doneness, simply take them out of the oven,
unwrap the foil—do this carefully so you don't burn yourself—and slide
a dinner knife into the beet. It's done if it easily cuts through the beet. If
it doesn't, just wrap it back up, and put it back in the oven. When they're
done, let the beets completely cool in the foil before slicing—and whatever you do, don't wear white.

3. Cut the whole, peeled clementines right across the tummy (horizon-
tally) into slices about ½-inch/12 mm thick so the slices resemble flowers. Cut the cooled beets the same thickness, and layer them across a
serving plate, fanning them as you do so. Drizzle a little E-Z French
Vinaigrette over the top, and sprinkle with some feta and fresh dill.

★ **COWGIRL TIP:** No time to roast beets? Just buy them pre-roasted.

ASPARAGUS *and*
AVOCADO SALAD

One spring, I took a bus to the outskirts of Paris with a group of journalists and Yannick Alleno, the Michelin three-star chef at Le Meurice, to a family asparagus farm that was about to go under (it didn't, thanks to marketing muscle by a start-up company aimed at promoting local producers and helping them sell their goods).

It was at the end of the six-week asparagus season, which begins in France around the end of April and ends around the first or second week in June. The family had been growing asparagus for generations and had, in fact, supplied asparagus to Napoleon III.

Picking asparagus isn't easy work, we all found out as we shimmied the funny-looking skinny spade into the earth, hoping to slice the stalk at the correct root in the octopus-like system below ground. Some of us caught on faster than others, but the fragility of this ancient crop, and that of its growers, resonated.

I've always looked forward to the arrival of asparagus each year as the first sign of spring, but now, I think about those farmers and how little time they have to harvest, and profit from, their crop.

I try to do my part and eat as much asparagus as I can.

ASPARAGUS AND AVOCADO SALAD

1 pound/500 grams of asparagus,
  ends trimmed and cut into 2-inch/5 cm pieces

olive oil

sea salt and pepper

1 avocado, cubed

1 tablespoon of chopped fresh cilantro

Lime-Cilantro Oil (recipe follows)

lime zest

a small wedge of Parmesan cheese

a small handful of toasted pistachios,
  roughly chopped

1. Preheat your broiler and line a cookie sheet with foil.

2. Put your asparagus pieces on the cookie sheet. Add a little olive oil, a bit of sea salt and pepper, and toss it all together. Slide into the oven and broil just until the tips of the asparagus tips begin to brown. Remove from the oven and let them cool.

3. Get out a medium-size bowl and gently mix your asparagus, avocado pieces, and cilantro with a big drizzle (about 2 tablespoons) of the Lime-Cilantro Oil. Top this off with a sprinkle of lime zest, a few shavings of Parmesan, and some crushed pistachios.

> ★ **DOUBLE-DUTY:** Add salmon, grilled scallops, or smoked salmon to your salad for a light dinner.

LIME-CILANTRO OIL
MAKES ABOUT ½ CUP/120 ML

a small handful of fresh cilantro, chopped
1 clove of garlic, minced
the zest of 1 lime
⅓ cup/75 ml of olive oil
sea salt and pepper

Put the first 4 ingredients in a jam jar, and shake. Salt and pepper to taste. Let this hang out for an hour, at least, before using. It'll keep for at least a week in the fridge.

THROW-TOGETHER SALAD

Here's a little something (Secret #1) that I don't often admit:
If most of the Paris grocery stores didn't have their silly closed-on-Sunday,
open-only-until-8 p.m.-the-rest-of -the-week hours*, I wouldn't be forced to
use what I have on hand, and I wouldn't come up with the recipes I do.

I could probably call this whole book Throw-Together Recipes: What I Made
When the Stores Were Already Closed or When I Was Too Lazy to Walk Down
the Street.

Not very catchy, though.

Secret #2: If you buy good produce—beautiful veggies and fruits that are
fresh—when you do make it to the store or the market, you'll have little
trouble coming up with ideas about what to do with them.

How do you decide what to buy? Secret #3: I buy what I already know that I
love, and in some cases, what I don't love yet but want to get to know a bit
better.

One night, I had these gorgeous ripe apricots in my bowl, which I'd intended
to make a pie with, but now they needed to be eaten right away. Everything
else—romaine, pecans, feta, chorizo—I had on hand, too.

The idea started with apricots, and the rest came together easily, without a
thought of going to the store for a forgotten ingredient.

Besides, it was already too late for that.

* I'm happy to report that my neighborhood Franprix is now open until 9 p.m.
most nights.

THROW TOGETHER SALAD

MAKES 4 SERVINGS

16 thin slices of chorizo or other
   spicy cured sausage

1 head of romaine lettuce, cut into
   2-inch/5 cm strips or roughly torn

2 ripe apricots, pits removed and
   cut into 8 slices each

3/4 cup/75 grams of pecans, toasted
   and roughly chopped

1 to 2 tablespoons of crumbed feta

a big splash of balsamic vinegar

olive oil

sea salt and pepper

1. Fry up your chorizo until crisp in a skillet, just as you would with bacon, and let it drain on paper towels.

2. Put the romaine, apricots, pecans, and feta in a big bowl. Add the crispy chorizo. Right before serving, splash on some balsamic vinegar and olive oil, along with a bit of sea salt and pepper. Toss and serve.

★ **COWGIRL TIP:** Keep your nuts in the freezer, and they'll stay fresh for months.

★ **SWAP IT:** No chorizo? No big deal. Just use bacon or ham instead.

TEXAS PICKUP
SALAD

In the 1970s, Texas was coming into its own. It had its own magazine, *Texas Monthly*, a new restaurant in Dallas with a menu built around chili, the state's most famous and well-loved dish, and it wouldn't be long until Dean Fearing would arrive and put Southwestern cuisine on the world's culinary map.

A half-hour north, my hometown of Denton was pushing culinary boundaries, too.

Next to a laundromat and across from the tennis courts at what is now the University of North Texas, Texas Pickup served an unheard-of salad: On a dinner plate, piled high with crispy iceberg lettuce, there was chili, shredded cheddar, and Fritos. On top of it all, a river of the new white dressing that you made with buttermilk and mayonnaise, called Ranch.

It was the most exotic dish to hit Denton since the Denny's on I-35 introduced the bacon-cheeseburger, something that my family would pile into the station wagon for on special occasions.

In high school, my friend Melanie and I often played tennis at the courts across from Texas Pickup, and afterward, we'd both order this salad. I don't remember when or why, even, but Texas Pickup eventually closed, and I forgot all about this salad.

Until I moved to Paris, and began playing tennis again. A Pavlovian response kicked in, and I found myself craving this salad. I now bring Fritos back from Texas just to make it.

TEXAS PICKUP SALAD

MAKES 2 DINNER-SIZE SALADS

2 cups/500 grams of Texas Chili (p.320)

1 head of romaine, sliced into strips 2-inches/
   5 cm wide or roughly torn

3 ounces/100 grams of grated cheddar cheese

2 big handfuls of Fritos

2 fat tomatoes, quartered

Jalapeño-Buttermilk Dressing (recipe follows)

Warm up your chili, then on each of 2 of your biggest dinner plates, simply layer: a big handful of romaine, a cup of chili, some cheddar cheese, and as many Fritos as you'd like. Place the tomato quarters all around the edges of the plate, and pass the jar of Jalapeño-Buttermilk dressing. I like to let the cheese melt on top of the chili before I add the dressing.

JALAPEÑO-CILANTRO BUTTERMILK DRESSING

MAKES ABOUT 1 ½ CUPS/360 ML

1 shallot, finely chopped

2 pickled jalapeños, finely chopped

a big pinch of sea salt and pepper

1 tablespoon of chopped chives

1 tablespoon of chopped fresh cilantro,
   plus more for garnish

½ cup/120 ml of good mayonnaise, such as Hellmann's

½ cup/120 ml of crème fraîche or sour cream

½ cup/120 ml of buttermilk

Whisk together the first 5 ingredients and let rest for about 10 minutes. Add the mayo, crème fraîche, and buttermilk, and taste for seasonings. Cover and put in the fridge for a half-hour before serving.

END OF WINTER SALAD

I hate to talk trash about the produce in France, but I've noticed a rather large oversight.

There are no collard greens. No turnip greens. Or mustard greens, either. And you can forget about kale, the curly dark leafy of the moment.

But we do have Swiss chard and spinach here, which I often use together or interchangeably. It's not the same as *greens* greens, but they're both dark and leafy, so I think that counts for something.

I love Swiss chard and spinach, so much so that I came up with this recipe one winter when I was craving a salad but wanted something more filling.

What I got was loads of texture, with plenty of contrast and balance. Nutty barley. Sweet white raisins. The salty bite of Pecorino Romano cheese. The crunch of toasted walnuts. All tossed together with the Swiss chard and spinach. It's super-healthy, but don't let that put you off. In fact, you may not even want to mention it, because every time I do, X just rolls his eyes.

END OF WINTER SALAD

MAKES 6 SERVINGS

1 cup/190 grams of dried barley

1 big bunch of Swiss chard

2 big handfuls of fresh spinach,
  the woodsy stalks removed

olive oil

1 shallot, finely chopped

sea salt and pepper

a pinch of ground nutmeg

the zest of ½ lemon

a big pinch of red pepper flakes

a small handful of white raisins

a small handful of walnuts, toasted
  then roughly chopped

a small wedge of Pecorino Romano cheese

1. Put 4 cups/1 liter of salted water on to boil, and when it's ready, add the
   barley, reduce the heat to a simmer, and cover. Set your timer for 45 minutes. When it buzzes, let the barley rest in the pot for 10 minutes or so,
   then pour it into a colander to drain.

2. Remove the stalks from your Swiss chard and roughly cut the leaves into
   1-inch/2.5 cm strips. Rinse these well. Ditto with your spinach.

3. Drizzle some olive oil into your largest skillet, toss in the shallots, and
   turn the heat to medium-low. Let this cook for a few minutes, then add
   all of your Swiss chard and spinach along with a big pinch of salt and
   pepper, and give it a stir—just like spinach, Swiss chard shrinks like
   crazy, so don't worry if it seems like you've got too much for your skillet;
   it'll work just fine. Now add the nutmeg, lemon zest, and red pepper
   flakes, and keep stirring until the Swiss chard is just ever so slightly
   wilted—just like spinach, it'll keep cooking once it's off the heat. Drain

the chard-spinach mixture in a colander to remove the excess water.

4. Put your chard-spinach mixture and barley in a large bowl and give it a good toss. Add the raisins and walnuts and shave lots of curls of Pecorino Romano over right before serving. I like this best warm, but it's great at room temperature, too.

★ **COWGIRL TIP:** Swiss chard is part of the beet family, and the colors—white, yellow, and the red-leafed—have a similar taste structure. The red are the sweetest, the yellow slightly less so, and the white, the least sweet of the bunch.

★ **SWAP IT**: No Swiss chard? Just use all spinach instead. Kale or any other kind of greens would work great, too.

ROASTED BUTTERNUT SQUASH, SPINACH, *and* BACON SALAD

In the dead of winter when the entire city of Paris has turned a gloomy brownish gray, including the veggies at the market, where all I see is a sea of mushrooms, potatoes, and onions—I want color. I want something bright.

In Paris, winter means *potimarron*, the little pumpkin that tastes like chestnuts; sunny yellow spaghetti squash, if you're lucky enough to find one; and the always cheerful, widely available butternut squash, itself a reason to love winter. Its yellow-orange insides remind me of marigolds.

The first winter I made this squash salad, it was one of the coldest winters on record; the city was covered in snow by mid-December. Not particularly salad weather, but this isn't any old salad. The roasted butternut's still warm, the bacon crispy, and the spinach, a willing accomplice to it all.

ROASTED BUTTERNUT SQUASH, SPINACH, AND BACON SALAD

MAKES 2 DINNER-SIZE OR 4 FIRST-COURSE SALADS

1 small butternut squash, peeled, seeded,
  and cut into 1-inch/2.5 cm cubes

olive oil

sea salt and pepper

2 big handfuls (about 5 ounces/140 grams)
  of baby spinach

4 slices of cooked bacon, crumbled

Apple Cider Vinaigrette (recipe follows)

about 2 ounces/55 grams of fresh goat cheese, crumbled

1. Preheat your broiler.

2. Put the squash pieces on a foil-lined cookie sheet, and drizzle them with some olive oil, salt and pepper, and toss with your hands and make sure they're evenly coated. Slide the cookie sheet into the oven for about 15 minutes, checking and turning the pan around if necessary. When the edges of the squash turn brown, they're done.

3. Assemble your salad while the squash is still warm. Just get out a big salad bowl, and add your spinach, still-warm squash pieces, and bacon bits. Add some of the vinaigrette on top and toss (you may not need all of the vinaigrette). Crumble the goat cheese on top and serve right away.

> ★ **SWAP IT**: Instead of butternut squash, roast some pumpkin or acorn squash, or even sweet potato.

APPLE CIDER VINAIGRETTE
MAKES ¾ CUP/180 ML

1 shallot, finely chopped
¼ cup/60 ml of apple cider vinegar
1 tablespoon of grainy Dijon mustard
sea salt and pepper
½ cup/120 ml of grapeseed oil

In an old jam jar, add your minced shallot, apple cider vinegar, and grainy mustard along with a pinch of sea salt and pepper. Give it a shake and let this let rest for 10 minutes. Add the grapeseed oil, shake again, and taste for seasonings. You can store your vinaigrette in the fridge for a few days.

ASIAN CHICKEN SALAD with GINGER-LIME VINAIGRETTE

I love Asian food—Thai, Vietnamese, Japanese, Chinese, Korean, you name it—and my idea of a fun afternoon is going for a Bo Bun lunch at one of the places in the 13th arrondissement, one of Paris' two Chinatowns, then hitting Tang Frères, the Walmart-size grocery store for all things Asian, and filling up my basket with limes, knobs of ginger, bunches of cilantro, Thai chiles, and fresh tofu. The place is a madhouse with so many people shopping that you can hardly squeeze by each other, but it's such an adventure, I just ignore my own avoid-crowds rule and go for it.

Tang Frères reminds me of an Asian version of the Fiesta grocery store that I used to go to in my neighborhood in Dallas. It was like crossing the border into Mexico, with fresh tortillas and sugar-coated *pan de huevo* at the front of the store and *cabrito* near the back. More proof that food can take you places, and you don't even have to leave your own city.

This salad's my fast train to an Asian dinner without having to go to the other side of town. I came up with this as a way to use leftover chicken. Now I often roast chicken just so I can make this the next day. I love the bright mango, the crunchy cabbage, and the light lime-ginger vinaigrette that pulls it all together.

But the best thing about this salad just may be its practicality. There's absolutely nothing to cook.

ASIAN CHICKEN SALAD WITH GINGER-LIME VINAIGRETTE

MAKES 4 SERVINGS

3.5 ounces/100 grams of arugula

6 ounces/170 grams of shredded purple cabbage, green cabbage, or a mix of the two

1 1/4 cups/225 grams of leftover shredded chicken from Easy Roast Chicken (p.265)

1 avocado, cubed

1/2 of a ripe mango, cut into small chunks

a handful of fresh cilantro, chopped

1/2 cup/35 grams of sliced almonds, toasted

Ginger-Lime Vinaigrette (recipe follows)

sesame seeds

Put everything but the Ginger-Lime Vinaigrette in a large bowl. Right before serving, add the vinaigrette, gently toss, and sprinkle with sesame seeds.

GINGER-LIME VINAIGRETTE

MAKES ABOUT 1/2 CUP/120 ML

2 teaspoons of soy sauce

1 tablespoon of rice vinegar

the juice of 1 lime

a big pinch of ginger powder

a big pinch of red pepper flakes

1/4 cup/60 ml of canola oil, grapeseed oil, or another light, flavorless oil

Put everything in a jar; give it a shake and taste for seasoning. Let rest for 10 minutes or so before serving.

DEEP SOUTH SALAD

I love the Italian bread salad, *panzanella*, in the summertime, and this salad's a hopped-up, Deep South version of that.

Like panzanella, this salad's a great way to use up leftovers in the summertime, but instead of stale *pane Toscana*, it gets its heft from black-eyed peas. If you're lucky, there's an abundant summer crop of juicy, sweet tomatoes that you need to do something with because fresh tomatoes are the heart and soul of this dish.

Add some crispy bacon, crunchy pecans, and a hot bacon dressing to pull it all together, and I'm right back where I came from, catching fireflies in jars at sunset and running around barefoot, wet grass between my toes.

DEEP SOUTH SALAD

MAKES 2 DINNER-SIZE OR 4 FIRST-COURSE SALADS

4 slices of bacon

about 3 cups/360 grams of Jalapeño
Cornbread croutons (see p.210)

3 cups/750 grams of Mom's Black-Eyed
Peas (p.209), or you may used canned

a handful of cherry tomatoes, quartered

two big handfuls of arugula or baby spinach

a couple of green onions, sliced (white part only)

1 clove of garlic, minced

3 tablespoons of sherry vinegar

the juice of ½ lemon

2 teaspoons of Dijon mustard

2 teaspoons of honey

sea salt and pepper

½ cup/120 ml of grapeseed oil

a handful of toasted pecans, roughly chopped

1. Fry your bacon until it's crisp, leaving 2 tablespoons of the bacon grease
   in the skillet. Put the bacon on paper towels to drain.

2. Meanwhile, put the cornbread croutons, black-eyed peas, cherry tomatoes, arugula, and green onions in a big salad bowl. Crumble the bacon over
   the salad.

3. Shake up the garlic, sherry vinegar, lemon juice, mustard, honey, and
   salt and pepper in an old jam jar. Let this rest for 10 minutes, then add
   the grapeseed oil and shake again.

4. Reheat the bacon grease in the skillet and when it's warm, whisk in the
   dressing. Let it cook for about a minute, then pour over your salad and
   toss. Top with pecans and serve immediately.

CHAPTER 5

Tacos, Tarts, and Tartines

What do tacos, tarts, and tartines have in common?

They're all easy to assemble. Simple to serve. Food that's fast, but doesn't come through your car window in a paper sack.

If I've got tortillas in the house, and if I'm hungry, the first thing I'll think of is a taco. An anything-that-I've-got-in-the-fridge taco. Eggs, ham, leftover chicken, veggies from the night before. I have eaten more tacos than sandwiches in my day, but what's a taco anyway but a folded-over Mexican sandwich that's made with a tortilla?

In France, *le sandwich* is commonly eaten without the top layer of bread, turning it into *la tartine*, which sounds much fancier than it is. But it is much more French to eat a topless sandwich on a plate, with a sharp knife and a fork—the way everything, including pizza and hamburgers, is eaten here. (X also eats tacos, and even nachos, like this, and when he does, I try to look the other way.) Ham-stuffed baguettes aside, this isn't an eat-with-your-hands kind of place.

Tarts are the French answer to what to make for dinner when you're short on ideas, low on eggs (they only require a few), and don't have much time. They are deceptively easy, which I mention because they look more difficult to make than an American pie; in fact, they are far simpler. There is no edge to crimp; you just roll out the dough, put it in the tart pan, and let it hang over as much as you want. Or, if you want to be neat, just pass your rolling pin over the top, so the edges are even. Because tart pans are much more shallow than pie pans, what's inside of them cooks much more quickly. Plus, tarts are versatile. Like tacos, they can be filled with all sorts of interesting things. They travel well. They can be eaten warm or cold. They're great for picnics as well as weeknight dinners. Have I sold you on buying a tart pan yet?

CORONA BEER-BRAISED BRISKET TACOS

My remedy for jet lag? Tacos and beer.

When the plane touches down in Dallas after the 11-hour flight from Paris, my mom picks me up at the airport and we drive straight to Mazatlan, a family-run Tex-Mex joint in an old Dairy Queen, right next to the Holiday Lanes bowling alley, in my hometown of Denton. I order an icy Negra Modelo, and we stuff ourselves with warm tortilla chips, salsa, and queso until the brisket tacos arrive. Knowing that I'll soon be sitting in a brown Naugahyde booth with Mom, eating my favorite tacos, is what gets me through the long plane ride home.

I try to get back to Texas as often as I can, but sometimes, the in-between-visits time stretches a bit too long.

A few years ago, with homesickness setting in and no plane ticket in hand, I got desperate, so I figured I'd just make my own. Brisket and corn tortillas. How hard could this be?

Well, harder than you'd think. Brisket doesn't exist in France. They don't cut up cows—or anything, for that matter—the way we do back home. Whereas we have about a dozen different cuts of beef, in France, there are more than thirty, so it wasn't a simple matter of translating the word brisket into its French equivalent, because there was no such thing. So I printed out diagrams of American butchery cuts and French ones, too, and stuffed them in my bag. I wrote down the words *paleron, macruese,* and *jumeau*, all French cuts that are in the same upper-shoulder area as brisket, and I went down the street to the butcher to try to explain. What I wanted, and how I was going to cook it—not even Rosetta Stone had enough French instruction to make sure I got a piece of meat that would work the same way brisket would.

Thinking about that conversation with the butcher still makes my head hurt.

Luckily, Corona was surprisingly easy to find and needed no translation.

CORONA BEER-BRAISED BRISKET

SERVES 6 TO 8

Vegetable or olive oil
sea salt and pepper
2 to 3 pounds/1 to 1½ kilos of beef brisket
3 onions, sliced into half-moons
8 cloves of garlic, minced
1 bottle of Corona beer
6 to 8 Corn Tortillas (p.315) or you may use store-bought
Pico de Gallo (p.319)
Holy Guacamole! (p.318)

1. Position a rack in the lowest part of the oven and preheat your oven to 300°F/150°C.

2. Heat some oil in a big Dutch oven over medium-high heat, and while it's warming up, generously salt and pepper your brisket on both sides. When the pot's hot, go ahead and brown your meat—on the top, bottom, and all sides—then take it out and let it rest on a plate.

3. Turn the heat down to medium-low and add your onions and garlic to the pot, scraping the brown bits off the bottom with your wooden spoon. If the onions stick to the pot, just add a little more oil. Let this cook for a couple of minutes, and then add about three-quarters of the bottle of beer. Keep scraping the bottom so you can get all of the little crunchy bits. Once you're finished, turn the heat off and put the meat back in the pot. See where the beer lands on the meat—it should be about one-third up the side from the bottom. No more, no less. If it's not, add a bit more beer, and if you've hit it just right, the rest is for you. Thirsty work, cooking.

4. Now, one last thing, and this is a great trick: Tear off a big piece of parchment paper and press it right down into your pot, directly onto the brisket and the juices. Even though we're putting a tight lid on the pot before it goes into the oven, this helps push more of the moisture down back into the meat, which will make it even that much more tender. It'll

also make the beer-onion sauce more concentrated and flavorful.

5. Cover the pot and slide it onto the lowest oven rack and set the timer for 15 minutes, so you can check back and see if it's simmering. If it is, great; if not, adjust the temperature. Let this cook for 2 to 2½ hours, checking on it every now and then, and pulling it out to flip the meat over. It's ready when it just takes the gentle push of a wooden spoon for the meat to fall apart. Let it cool in the pot, with the lid on, for a couple of hours. Once it's cool, shred your meat and keep it in the juices. Slide it into the fridge until the next day.

6. To warm up your brisket for tacos, preheat your oven to 350°F/175°C. Put the meat in a casserole dish with some of the juices, cover with foil, and let it warm through for 30 to 45 minutes. Serve with Corn Tortillas , Pico de Gallo , and Holy Guacamole!

★ **ADVANCE PLANNING:** Make this the day before you want to eat it, and you'll be happy that you did. Like any braise, the magic happens overnight, after cooking and cooling, and the meat itself takes on the flavors of what you've cooked it with, and becomes even more tender.

TACOS AL PASTOR

When I'm back in Texas, I'm on a mission to eat as much Tex-Mex as I can. Which means tacos for breakfast, tacos for lunch, and if I can swing it, tacos for dinner.

One of my favorite places in Dallas to get tacos is Fuel City, the combination truck stop and taqueria about a half-mile from the county jail. Which seems fitting, actually. I'm sure the first thing I'd want when I got out of jail would be a taco. And maybe a shower.

Fuel City is legendary and has been hailed as having some of the best tacos in the state. I've not yet tasted all of the tacos in Texas, but these are at the top of my list. Plus, they're super-cheap—just $1.40 apiece.

They've got a whole range of breakfast tacos and picadillo, barbacoa, and beef and chicken fajita tacos, too. I usually go for the tacos al pastor, served, like the rest of the tacos at Fuel City, with fresh cilantro, chopped jalapeño, finely diced white onion, salsa, and lime.

A street-vendor staple in Mexico City, pork cooked *al pastor* is slow-roasted on Middle Eastern shawarma-style rotisseries, so the meat is super-moist. Besides the non-traditional way of cooking there's the taste itself— smoke and fire from the chiles (which give this a warm orangey color) and a sweetness that perfectly balances the heat, which comes from an unexpected source—pineapple.

A few weeks after a Fuel City taco fill-up in Texas, I found myself back in Paris, with an al pastor craving that wouldn't go away. With nary a taco stand in sight, and certainly not a truck stop selling tacos, I decided to give it a go myself.

Since we're not allowed to have grills in Paris, I nixed the marinating in pineapple, then grilling the pork idea, opting to let the oven do the work instead.

And work it did. One bite and I was back at Fuel City, standing in line with the construction workers, suited-up attorneys, and just-released inmates, eating my taco, leaning on the hood of my mom's green truck.

TACOS AL PASTOR

SERVES 6 TO 8

Vegetable or olive oil
sea salt and pepper
2 to 3 pounds/1 to 1½ kilos of pork shoulder
2 onions, 1 sliced into half-moons and 1 finely chopped
4 cloves of garlic, minced
⅓ cup/75 ml of orange-flavored liqueur, such as Cointreau
¾ cup/180 ml of Adobo Salsa (p.323)
1 cup/240 ml of water
½ of a fresh pineapple, cut into 2-inch/5 cm chunks
2 teaspoons of cumin
1 teaspoon of dried oregano
6 to 8 Corn Tortillas (p.315) or you may use store-bought
a small handful of fresh cilantro, chopped
a few jalapeños, finely chopped
4 or 5 limes, sliced into wedges

1. Position a rack in the lowest part of the oven and preheat your oven to 300°F/150°C.

2. Drizzle some oil in a big Dutch oven over medium-high heat, and while it's warming up, generously salt and pepper your pork shoulder. When the pot's hot, go ahead and brown your meat—on the top, bottom, and all sides—then take it out and let it rest on a plate.

3. Turn your heat down to medium-low and add the half-moon onion slices, plus a little more oil if you need to. When the onions start to soften—it'll only take a minute or two—go ahead and add the garlic and give this a couple of stirs. When you smell the garlic, add your Cointreau and using your big wooden spoon, scrape all of the crunchy brown bits off of the bottom of the pot.

4. Whisk the Adobo Salsa with 1 cup of water and add this to the pot, along with the pineapple chunks, cumin, and oregano. I like to add another teaspoon of sea salt and pepper at this point, too. Turn off the heat and add your pork back to the pot. The liquid should come up to about one-third on the side of the meat.

5. Now, I'd like to introduce you to the secret to opening your oven to a juicy, perfectly cooked piece of braised meat: parchment paper. Just tear off a piece that'll fit down into the pot nicely, press it right onto your piece of pork, and then let it go up the sides a little bit. Don't worry, this doesn't need to be perfect. The idea is to push the moisture thrown off by the meat and the juices right back down, which will make the meat just that much more tender and the sauce more concentrated and flavorful.

6. Cover the pot and slide it onto the lowest oven rack and set your timer for 15 minutes, so you can check on its progress. It should be simmering, but not boiling. Adjust the temperature if you need to. Let this cook for 2-2½ hours, checking on it every now and then, and pulling the pot out and flipping the meat to the other side. It's ready when the meat falls away with a gentle push with your wooden spoon. Let this cool in the pot, with the lid on, for a couple of hours. Once it's cool, shred your meat and keep it in its juices in the fridge until the next day.

7. To warm up your pork for tacos, preheat your oven to 350°F/175°C. Put the pork and some of the sauce in a casserole dish, cover with foil, and let it warm through for 30 to 45 minutes. Serve with corn tortillas, chopped onion, cilantro, jalapeño, and lime wedges.

> ★ **COWGIRL TIP:** Cutting up a pineapple can be a sticky mess. To cut down on the cleanup, I slice mine on a dishtowel, right on top of my cutting board.

TACOS CARNITAS *with* PURPLE ROQUEFORT SLAW

Before I lived in France, I rarely ate pork. I guess after one too many dry, tasteless pork chops in my day, I simply gave up. Now, if there's pig *anything*—cheeks, belly, or just a plain old chop—on the menu, it's my first choice.

As much as I like to complain about the beef here (see p. 242), I've got nothing but good things to say about the pork. The French definitely know how to do pig.

I have eaten chops that are so tender and juicy I've wanted to cry, and enough *jambon de Paris, jambon de Bayonne, lardons*, and saucisson to build my very own pork Eiffel Tower. When X goes to the store, he always buys ham. With more than sixty different kinds of pre-sliced packaged ham at the grocery store to choose from, who can blame him?

This recipe isn't made from the finest cut of pork, and it's not meant to be. But I daresay these crispy-on-the-outside and juicy-and-piggy-tasting-on-the-inside French pork Mexican carnitas are some of the best that I've ever tasted anywhere. Including Mexico City.

It's not always easy trying to replicate recipes over here, because the ingredients and products are often not the same. Sometimes this turns out to be a very good thing.

TACOS CARNITAS WITH
PURPLE ROQUEFORT SLAW

SERVES 6 TO 8

Vegetable or olive oil

2 to 3 pounds/1 to 1½ kilos of pork shoulder

1 onion, chopped

4 cloves of garlic, minced

1 cinnamon stick

1 teaspoon of cumin

½ teaspoon of dried oregano

1 teaspoon of smoky Spanish paprika*
  or ancho chile powder

sea salt and pepper

6 to 8 Corn Tortillas (p.315) or you may use store-bought.

Purple Roquefort Slaw, recipe follows

4 or 5 limes, sliced into wedges

1. Position a rack in the lowest part of the oven and preheat your oven to 300°F/150°C.

2. Pour a little oil in a big Dutch oven, set it over medium-high heat, and when it's hot, put the pork in, and sear it on each side. When the pork is brown and crispy all over, take it out and let it rest on a plate and turn the heat down to medium. Toss in the onions and garlic and more oil if you need to and stir them around with your wooden spoon, scraping the bottom to get all of the browned bits. Once the onions have cooked for a minute or two, add 1 cup/240 ml of water and keep stirring along the bottom, so you can get every last bit. Go ahead and add the pork back to the pot. Check the water level—it should reach one-third up the pork from the bottom. If it doesn't, add a little more. The idea here is not to cook the meat in too much liquid.

3. Toss in the cinnamon stick, cumin, oregano, Spanish paprika, a big pinch of salt and some pepper. Give it a stir, then turn off the heat.

4. One last step: Tear off a big piece of parchment paper and press it right down into your pot, directly onto the pork and the juices. Even though we're putting a tight lid on the pot before it goes into the oven, this helps push more of the moisture down back into the meat, which will make it even that much more tender. And it makes for a great, super-concentrated sauce.

5. Cover the pot, slide it onto the lowest oven rack and set the timer for 15 minutes, so you can check back and see if it's simmering. If it is, great; if not, adjust the temperature. Let this cook for 2-2½ hours, checking every now and then, and pulling it out to flip the meat over. It's ready when it just takes the gentle push of a wooden spoon for the meat to fall apart. Let it cool in the pot, with the lid on, for a couple of hours. Then refrigerate until the next day.

6. When you want to eat your carnitas, preheat your broiler, and position a rack in the middle of the oven. Once the oven's nice and hot, put your pork, along with the juices and onions, in a baking dish (you don't want to cover this) and slide it on in. Let this go for 15 to 20 minutes, keeping a close eye on it so it doesn't burn, and when it's brown and crispy, it's ready. Serve on fresh corn tortillas with a heap of Purple Roquefort Slaw and lime wedges.

* I use Santo Domingo brand "agridulce" smoky paprika, which is simply smoky, not hot.

PURPLE ROQUEFORT SLAW
MAKES 6 TO 8 SERVINGS

1 shallot, finely chopped
¼ cup/60 ml of apple cider vinegar
1 teaspoon of Dijon mustard
sea salt and pepper
½ cup/120 ml of grapeseed oil, canola oil,
   or another light oil
½ head of a purple cabbage, thinly sliced

the juice of about ½ lime

2½ ounces/75 grams of Roquefort cheese, crumbled

a handful of fresh cilantro, roughly chopped

1. Put your shallot, apple cider vinegar, Dijon mustard, and a nice pinch of salt and pepper in an old jam jar and give it a shake. Let it rest for 10 minutes, then add the grapeseed oil and shake again. Put the sliced cabbage in a large bowl. Pour the vinaigrette over the chopped cabbage and toss. Pop this in the fridge for a few hours or overnight.

2. Right before you're ready to serve this, give the cabbage and dressing another toss, add the lime juice, Roquefort, and cilantro and toss again. Taste for seasonings.

SPINACH, POTATO, *and* CARAMELIZED ONION TACOS

One kilo (a little over two pounds) is the maximum amount of spinach I can stuff into the kitchen sink.

My kitchen sink, like the rest of the features of my Paris kitchen, is small. It is not a double, and it is just eight inches deep. Cookie sheets and Silpats simply won't fit, so I wash them in the bathtub, where I have a hand-held sprayer (which most Parisian kitchens lack, along with garbage disposals). So far, I have not had to resort to washing spinach in the bathtub and doing the Lucy Ricardo grape-stomp.

But you hear stories. People wash all sorts of things in their bathtubs here.

Thankfully, once it's rinsed of all its dirt, spinach can be put in a towel-lined colander on the countertop to drain. Yes, I know. It's a process. It takes some time. And some precious kitchen real estate. But for those of you who have a normal-size kitchen with a large, deep sink, or better yet, a double sink, this really isn't that big of a deal, now is it?

Spinach cooks up in no time. No time at all. Which is great not just for ease of cooking but because spinach is high in nutritional value and extremely rich in antioxidants, especially if it's fresh, steamed, or quickly boiled. It couldn't be easier: I get out my biggest, deepest, made-in-the-U-S-of-A skillet (which dwarfs my little four-burner, BTU-challenged gas stove), stuff it with my spinach, and let it go.

If I can make this in my silly little kitchen, the rest of you can, too. No excuses.

SPINACH, POTATO, AND CARAMELIZED ONION TACOS

MAKES 8 TO 10 TACOS

1 pound/500 grams of red-skinned potatoes,
  cut into 2-inch/5 cm pieces

olive oil

sea salt and pepper

2 onions, sliced into half-moons,
  plus ½ of an onion, chopped

1 clove of garlic, minced

20 ounces/600 grams of fresh spinach,
  washed and stems removed

a pinch of ground nutmeg

about ¼ teaspoon of lemon zest

a pinch of cayenne pepper

8 to 10 Wheat or Corn Tortillas (p.312 and p.315)
  or you may use store-bought

a handful of crumbled queso fresco or feta cheese

3 or 4 limes, sliced into wedges

Taqueria Salsa (p.316), or your favorite bottled
  salsa, such as Valentina or Cholula

1. Preheat the oven to 450°F/230°C, toss your potatoes on a parchment-lined cookie sheet, and drizzle some olive oil over them. Sprinkle a bit of sea salt and pepper on top, and mix it all up with your hands. Pop into the oven for 30 to 45 minutes, making sure to check them frequently and flip to the other side about halfway through—check at 20 minutes—when the edges start to brown.

2. While the potatoes are roasting, make your caramelized onions. Get out a big skillet and add your onion slices and some olive oil, and turn the heat to medium-low. Cook the onions slowly, for about 30 to 45 minutes, stirring every now and then, until they're brown and caramelized. The

slower these cook, the better they'll be.

3. Now, cook your spinach. This won't take any time at all. Put a little olive oil in your largest skillet, along with the chopped onion and minced garlic. Cook over medium-low for just a few minutes, until the onion begins to become translucent. Now add the spinach, nutmeg, lemon zest, pinch of cayenne, sea salt and pepper, and cook only until the spinach begins to wilt. Remove from the heat and put straight into a colander, so the water can drain off the spinach.

4. It's taco time. Warm up your tortillas either on a comal, one by one, or stacked and wrapped in foil for about 10 minutes in a hot (375°F/190°C) oven. For each taco, simply layer a bit of spinach and potatoes across the middle of the warm tortilla, then top with a few caramelized onions and a bit queso fresco or feta. Serve with lime, and pass the salsa, *por favor*.

★ **COWGIRL TIP:** Caramelized onions are great to have on hand, so you may want to double up on these. They're great on sandwiches and pizzas, added to soups, and stirred into omelettes or pasta.

★ **DOUBLE-DUTY:** On its own, the spinach makes a great side dish for Salmon with Kalamata Olive-Basil Salsa (p.269).

FISH TACOS
with MANGO-AVOCADO SALSA

Fish tacos aren't as big in Texas as you might think given that it sits right on the Gulf. We do eat a lot of shrimp in Texas, and a whole lot of catfish, so you'd think that someone would've pushed this idea a little bit more.

Paris is big on fish of all sorts, and I love buying fish here. The *poissonniers* are always happy to take a whole fish, that's lying on the ice display, and cut it into fillets for you, right there, while you wait. It's that fresh.

Reminds me of fishing for catfish with my dad at my grandfather's lake in Oklahoma. Those catfish were particularly fond of chicken fat, and we'd bait the hooks of our bamboo poles and wait for the little red-and-white bobber to go under. We'd pull in the whiskered white-bellied fish, and they'd flop around on the ground for a while, until they didn't anymore. Back at the house, Daddy would clean the fish with a Bowie knife and a garden hose. Then Mom would fry them up, hush puppies on the side.

These tacos are inspired by all of that— the fresh fish I see every day here, the crunchy cornmeal crust that my mom made, the afternoons spent fishing with my dad. And my own tendency to turn just about anything into a taco.

FISH TACOS WITH MANGO-AVOCADO SALSA

MAKES 10 TO 12 TACOS

1 mango, chopped

1 avocado, chopped

2 tablespoons of finely chopped red onion

1 jalapeño, finely chopped

a small handful of fresh cilantro, chopped

the juice of 1 lime

a few pinches of sea salt, divided

½ cup/80 grams of cornmeal

¼ teaspoon of cayenne pepper

1 pound/500 grams of medium-firm
   white fish fillets, such as halibut,
   cut into 2-inch/5 cm chunks

¼ cup /60 ml of buttermilk

corn oil, for frying

10 to 12 Corn Tortillas (p.315)
   or you may use store-bought

3 to 4 limes, sliced into wedges, for serving

1. Gently toss together your mango, avocado, red onion, jalapeño, cilantro, and lime juice. Taste and add a pinch or two of salt.

2. Whisk together the cornmeal, cayenne, and big pinch of sea salt. Pour the buttermilk into a bowl. Dip your fish pieces in the buttermilk, and then roll them around in the cornmeal, and shake off the excess. Add just enough corn oil to the bottom of a large skillet to coat it and turn the heat to medium-high. When it's hot, add your fish, turning them when one side's brown—this whole process will only take a couple of minutes, since fish cooks quickly. Immediately top the fresh corn tortillas with a few pieces of fish, and pass the mango-avocado salsa and lime wedges.

TOMATO-
RICOTTA TART

It begins around the middle of May. The unfurling of blankets on any patch of grass or flat pedestrian-free spot in Paris. Along Avenue Foch stretching from Porte Dauphine to the Arc de Triomphe. In the expansive 2,137-acre Bois de Boulogne park. Up and down the Seine. Wine is uncorked and passed around and poured into plastic cups. Baguettes are torn. Pâté is sliced. Salads are tossed. And the eating begins.

And goes on for hours.

The French are particularly obsessed with *le pique-nique.*

And a picnic is not a *pique-nique* in Paris without a tomato tart. I once went to a picnic where there were four different ones—all slight variations on the simple combination of tomato, crust, and either cheese or mustard, or both. Yes, mustard. A thin layer of Dijon mustard, plus tomatoes, is the most common summer tart in France.

Too simple, you may be thinking. Tomatoes. Crust. Cheese.

Well, let me remind you about a little something called *la pizza.*

Which is sort of what I had in mind here. A free-form tart, one that doesn't require a tart pan, that could be rolled out into a thick or thin crust, smeared with herby ricotta, and topped with tomatoes. Great for picnics, if you happen to be in France, and perfect for your dinner table if you don't.

TOMATO-RICOTTA TART

MAKES ENOUGH FOR 4

Crust

2½ cups/300 grams of flour

½ teaspoon of sea salt

½ cup/120 ml of olive oil

¼ cup/60 ml of dry white wine,
   such as Sauvignon Blanc or Chardonnay

¼ cup/60 ml of whole milk

Filling

¾ cup/150 grams of Super-Quick Homemade Ricotta
   (recipe follows), or you may use store-bought

2 tablespoons of olive oil, plus a bit
   more for drizzling on top

about 1 teaspoon of chopped fresh basil, divided

about 1 teaspoon of fresh thyme leaves, divided

about 1 teaspoon of chopped fresh flat-leaf parsley, divided

sea salt and pepper

1 medium tomato, sliced

1. Make your tart dough. Whisk together the flour and salt; then add the olive oil, white wine, and milk, and mix until combined with a wooden spoon, your hands, or pulsed until it comes together in a food processor—this is a very easy dough. Cover the dough plastic wrap and put in the fridge for an hour.

2. Preheat the oven to 375°F/190°C, and while the oven's coming to temperature, mix up your homemade ricotta with the 2 tablespoons olive oil, about ½ teaspoon each of the fresh herbs, and a pinch of sea salt and pepper.

3. When you're ready to make your tart, on your floured work surface, roll out the dough to the desired shape and thickness—since we're not using a tart pan, it can be one large rectangle, or two, if you like your crust

super-thin, which I do. Don't worry too much about how this looks—we're going for rustic, not perfect.

4. Put the dough on a parchment-lined cookie sheet and prick the bottom a few times with a fork. Bake the tart shell for about 15 to 20 minutes or until it's firm but not browned. Remove from the oven and let cool for about 5 minutes.

5. Go ahead and spread the herby ricotta mixture all over the tart shell, then add the tomatoes, a bit of sea salt, pepper and olive oil over. Bake for 20 to 30 minutes, or until the tomatoes are cooked. Sprinkle the rest of the fresh herbs on top and serve.

SUPER-QUICK HOMEMADE RICOTTA
MAKES ABOUT 2 CUPS/500 GRAMS

4 cups/1 liter of milk
1 cup/240 ml of buttermilk
1 cup/240 ml of cream
a big pinch of sea salt

1. Cut out a piece of cheesecloth and lay it in a colander, set over a medium-size bowl.

2. Put the milk, buttermilk, cream, and salt in a large, heavy saucepan and turn the heat to medium-high. Stir every now and then so the milk doesn't scorch on the bottom of the pan. When it boils, reduce the heat to the lowest setting, and watch the curds rise to the surface. With a slotted spoon, gently remove the curds and put them in the cheesecloth-lined colander nearby. They'll continue to bubble up for about 5 minutes, then you can turn off the heat. Don't squeeze your curds with the cheesecloth; rather, just let them drain for 15 minutes—and voila!—you've got ricotta. Remove the cheesecloth and put your ricotta in a plastic container and keep it in the fridge. It's only good for about 2 days, so eat it right away.

TEX-MEX TART

I'm calling this a tart, but I think we all know what it really is.

Corn tortilla dough pressed into a French tart pan, then layered with refried black beans, shredded chicken, and lots of melty cheese.

A big nacho.

I always smile when I make this, just like I do when I pour cornbread batter into my madeleine pans, because I'm thinking, Ha! I know there's no one else in Paris right now making this with *this* pan. I know how silly it sounds, but I always take a special pleasure in discovering a new way to use something that's designed specifically for something else. It's a bit of defiant fun to fly in the face of convention, especially here.

You may have noticed that the French are not real big on change. This is an old country. People do things the same way they always have. There are rules. There is protocol. There is a *tu* form of *"you"* and a *vous* form of *"you"* and a time and a place for each. Convention isn't always an easy thing to navigate.

After I'd known X's family for a few years, I asked him if I could use the informal *tu* form with his parents, who had already been using it with me. "I can have a meeting with them and ask if you want," he said.

A meeting.

When I said that I wanted to have some people we'd met at the park over for dinner, he suggested we meet for a drink at a restaurant down the street instead. I asked him why. "This is just how we do things," he said.

I'm from Texas. And I can strike up a conversation with anyone, whether I know them or not. When I lived in Dallas, the checkers at Whole Foods hugged me when I walked in the door (probably because I was such a good customer, but still . . .). Here in Paris, X looks at me with horror when I greet the baristas at our neighborhood Starbucks with kisses on both cheeks. And quizzically when I serve him big nachos out of French tart pans. This, I explain to him, is just how I do things.

TEX-MEX TART

MAKES 1 (11-INCH/28 CM) TART

2½ cups/625 grams of masa

1 teaspoon of sea salt

1¼ cups /300 ml of hot water

3 cups/500 grams of cooked and drained
  Back in Black Beans (p.314), or you may use canned

2 tablespoons of lard, duck fat, or vegetable oil

1 clove of garlic, minced

1 teaspoon of cumin

¼ teaspoon of sea salt

2 cups/345 grams of shredded
  Easy Roast Chicken (p.265)

2 cups/120 grams of grated cheddar or
  Monterey Jack cheese

a small handful of fresh cilantro, chopped

Peach-Tomato Chipotle Salsa (recipe follows)

1. Preheat the oven to 375°F/190°C and line the bottom of an 11-inch/28 cm tart pan with parchment paper (I do this even with my nonstick tart pans).

2. Make your corn tortilla tart dough. Put the masa and sea salt in a food processor or whisk them together in a medium bowl. Slowly add the hot water and mix (or pulse in the processor) until combined. The dough should be firm, yet moist; not dry, crumbly, or sticky. With your fingers, press the dough right into your tart pan—I've rolled this out, too, but it's just as fast to do it this way. Cover the dough with a piece of parchment paper, add dried beans or pie weights, and bake for 15 minutes, or until the crust is firm. Remove from the oven, and let it cool.

3. Make your refried beans. In a medium bowl, smash up the drained black beans with a potato masher or hand blender. Get out one of your largest skillets, big enough to comfortably hold the beans, and add your lard, duck fat, or vegetable oil along with the minced garlic, and cook over medium heat for a minute or two, just until the garlic softens. Now, add the beans, cumin, and sea salt and cook and stir the beans until they are dry, about 5 minutes. Set them aside so they can cool.

4. To assemble the tart, evenly spread the beans on the bottom of the tart shell, then add the shredded chicken. Top with your shredded cheese. Cover loosely with foil and bake for 20 minutes. Then, remove the foil and bake for 10 more minutes, so the cheese gets bubbly. To serve, top with the chopped cilantro and a big spoonful of Peach-Tomato Chipotle Salsa, or just pass it around and let everyone add their own.

> ★ **DOUBLE-DUTY:** Sprinkled with a little queso fresco or feta, these refried beans make a great side for any of the tacos in this chapter.

PEACH-TOMATO CHIPOTLE SALSA
MAKES ABOUT 2 CUPS/ 230 GRAMS

1 large tomato, diced
1 large peach, diced
1 tablespoon of red onion, diced
the juice of $\frac{1}{2}$ lime (about 1 tablespoon)
1 canned chipotle in adobo
a pinch of sea salt
a small handful of fresh cilantro, chopped
(about 1 tablespoon)

Put all of the ingredients in a bowl. Let sit for an hour in the fridge before serving. Taste and adjust seasonings, if you need to.

> ★ **DOUBLE-DUTY:** This salsa also goes great with grilled fish, shrimp, and scallops.

SPINACH *and* ROQUEFORT TART

Given the choice, X would eat a ham and cheese pizza every night. Then he'd have a bowl of ice cream for dessert.

Other than the brief period when X declared himself a vegetarian, and vowed to eat lighter and healthier—a dalliance that lasted all of three weeks—it's been this way since I've known him. His favorite vegetable is a potato, which he loves best cooked in cream with cheese on top (*gratin dauphinois*) and served alongside a bloody steak, cooked *bleu*, with Roquefort sauce on the side. His Frenchness causes him to consume more dairy products on a daily basis than I ever imagined possible. We're talking enormous hunks of cheese in various degrees of stinkiness; cartons of yogurt, generously sweetened with swirls of raspberry jam, honey, or maple syrup; and the milkiest coffee that I've ever seen. (I tune my coffee with a splash of milk; not the other way around.)

French paradox or not, it seems to me that he's on the road straight to high-cholesterol land. But since my not-so-gentle suggestions have had little impact, I've got my own methods. I either hide veggies that X doesn't like in something that he won't be able to resist (Cauliflower Galettes, p.204; or Broccoli-Basil Soup, p.96), or I try to create something that he'll love by incorporating one of few veggies that he'll willingly eat. With enough Roquefort to entice him, I don't even have to resort to Popeye's muscles.

SPINACH AND ROQUEFORT TART

MAKES 1 (11-INCH/28 CM) TART

olive oil

1 shallot, finely chopped

16 ounces/450 grams of frozen chopped spinach, thawed

a big pinch of nutmeg

¼ teaspoon of lemon zest

sea salt and pepper

3 eggs

½ cup /120 ml of milk

5 fresh sage leaves, chopped

2 ounces/60 grams of Roquefort cheese, crumbled

1 Whole Wheat-Oatmeal tart crust, blind-baked
and cooled (recipe follows)

1. Preheat your oven to 375°F/190°C.

2. Pour a little bit of olive oil into your skillet, add the shallots, and turn the heat to medium-low. Let this cook just a few minutes, until the shallots become translucent.

3. Squeeze as much water out of the chopped spinach as you can (I use a potato ricer for this) and add this to the skillet. Toss in the nutmeg, lemon zest, sea salt and pepper and give it all a stir. Cook until it's warmed through, about 5 minutes; then pour the spinach mixture into a bowl to let it cool.

4. Whisk your eggs with the milk and the sage, and add a pinch of sea salt and pepper. Evenly spread the spinach all over the bottom of the tart shell, and sprinkle the Roquefort on top. Pour the egg mixture over this, and bake for 30 minutes or until the tart is set. Serve warm.

WHOLE WHEAT-OATMEAL TART CRUST

MAKES 1 (11-INCH/28 CM) TART SHELL

This recipe was inspired by one for a tart crust made with whole-wheat flour and olive oil that I found on Clotilde Desoulier's blogsite, Chocolate and Zucchini. I loved the idea of whole wheat because it's got such a great nutty taste, but using olive oil instead of butter is what really got my attention.

2 cups/250 grams of whole-wheat flour

¼ cup/50 grams of oatmeal (quick)

1 teaspoon of sea salt

¼ cup/60 ml of olive oil

1 tablespoon of honey

½ cup /120 ml of ice water

1. Line the bottom of an 11-inch/28 cm tart pan with a round of parchment paper (*très important*—this will keep your crust from sticking to the pan and tearing apart), and preheat your oven to 375°F/190°C.

2. In a medium bowl, whisk together the flour, oatmeal, and sea salt. Add the oil and honey and mix it up by hand—I sometimes use a big wooden spoon, but more often, just use my hands. It's easier, quicker, and one less thing to wash. Now add your ice water, little by little (you may not need all of it), and mix just until the dough comes together in a ball.

3. Roll out the dough on a lightly floured surface, lay it into the tart pan, and use your kitchen scissors to trim the hangover, leaving ½ inch/12 mm—it allows for shrinkage, plus it's prettier this way. Prick the bottom with a fork and refrigerate for an hour or pop in the freezer for 30 minutes (my favorite method, because it's faster), until the dough's nice and firm.

4. Blind bake your crust. Line the frozen crust with parchment and fill it up with pie weights or dry beans, making sure to push them tightly into the edges, where shrinkage can occur. Put the tart pan on a cookie sheet and bake for 20 minutes. Remove the weights and parchment, and bake for 10 more minutes, so the bottom cooks through. Let the tart shell cool completely before you fill it.

ROASTED BROCCOLI-RED BELL PEPPER TART

Four years of eating daily baguettes smeared with *fleur de sel* butter and raspberry jam and duck confit whenever I felt like it had finally caught up with me. My jeans were tight. Even my T-shirts had gotten snug. As much as I wanted to blame the French washer and dryer for shrinking my clothes, I couldn't. My clothes hadn't gotten smaller. I'd gotten bigger.

I needed to find balance again, in my body and in my eating. So I signed up for yoga classes, and I was back on the mat, faced with it all.

I wasn't about to give up all good things French, but I knew it wouldn't hurt— me or X, who'd been my chief food tester—to trim down a bit. To limit our baguette intake, cut back on the cheese, skip the *pains au chocolat* from the boulangerie across the street, and try to eat more veggies, fruits, and grains.

This tart is more veggies than custard filling, done purposely, so the egg-milk mixture (mostly whites and skinny milk) simply acts as glue to hold it all together. There's just enough cheese to give it a bit of richness and depth, and to make it seem like a regular tart, not part of *un régime*, or diet, which everyone always seems to be on around here.

ROASTED BROCCOLI-RED BELL PEPPER TART

MAKES 1 (11-INCH/28 CM) TART

1 medium head of broccoli, cut into florets

½ of a red bell pepper, cut into ½-inch/12 mm pieces

3 green onions, sliced (white part only)

olive oil

6 egg whites

¾ cup/180 ml of reduced fat milk, such as 2%

sea salt and pepper

2 cups/120 grams of grated cheddar, Monterey Jack, or your favorite melty cheese

1 Polenta Tart Crust, blind-baked and cooled (recipe follows)

1. Preheat your broiler, and line 2 big cookie sheets and 1 smaller one with foil. Toss the broccoli florets on one, the red bell pepper pieces on another, and the green onions on the small one. Drizzle about a tablespoon or so of olive oil over each batch of veggies, salt and pepper them, and give them a good toss with your hands—it's just easier this way.

2. Now that all of your veggies are prepped, go ahead and slide your broccoli into the oven, and let it cook for about 15 minutes, or until the florets are light brown. Do the same with the red bell peppers, and then the green onions. (These cook at slightly different times, which is why they're on separate cookie sheets—but they all cook quickly.)

3. Once the veggies are roasted, leave them on their pans to cool, and reduce your oven temperature to 375°F/190°C.

4. In a medium bowl, mix up the egg whites, milk, and salt and pepper.

5. Assemble your tart. First, lay as many broccoli florets as you can into the tart shell. Then add the cheese, and all or as much of the red bell pepper as you'd like, and top with the onions. Gently pour the eggy-milky mixture

over the veggies. You'll probably need to use your fingers to squish the cheese down a bit between the broccoli florets. Put the tart on a foil-lined cookie sheet (in case of spillage, this will make for an easy cleanup), and slide into the oven for 30 to 45 minutes, or until the tart is set. Let cool 10 minutes before serving.

POLENTA TART CRUST

MAKES 1 (11-INCH/28 CM) TART SHELL

$1^3/_4$ cups/270 grams of flour

$^3/_4$ cup/125 grams of yellow cornmeal or polenta

1 teaspoon of sea salt

$^1/_4$ cup /60 ml of olive oil

1 tablespoon of honey

$^1/_4$ cup/60 ml of ice water

1. Line the bottom of an 11-inch/28 cm tart pan with a round of parchment paper—very important, so your tart crust doesn't stick—and preheat your oven to 375°F/190°C.

2. Whisk together your flour, cornmeal, and sea salt. Add the oil and honey and mix it up. Pour in the water bit by bit, adding just enough for the dough to come together.

3. Roll out the dough out on a lightly floured surface, and gently lay it into your tart pan. Snip the crust edges with your kitchen scissors, leaving a dough hangover of about $^1/_2$ inch/12 mm. Refrigerate for an hour or simply pop in the freezer (which I often do) until firm, for about 30 minutes.

4. Blind bake your crust. Line the chilled crust with parchment and fill it up with pie weights or dry beans, making sure to push them tightly into the edges, where shrinkage can occur. Put the tart pan on a cookie sheet and bake for 20 minutes. Remove the weights and parchment, and bake for 10 more minutes, so the bottom cooks through. Let the tart shell cool completely before you fill it.

ROASTED
VEGGIE MELT

For a long time, I've had a love-hate relationship with eggplant. Loved eating it, hated making it.

I'd sliced, salted, and drained it; then wiped off the salt, just like I was supposed to, to remove the eggplant's bitterness. I don't know if it worked or not: I always ended up with soggy, salty eggplant that I couldn't eat. So I nixed the salt and tried roasting it, without oil. My eggplant was dry and spongy.

I eventually gave up.

Then I moved to France, where eggplant, along with zucchini and red bell peppers—ratatouille's key ingredients—was prolific, and I knew I couldn't avoid it any longer. I had to figure eggplant out.

Turns out, the French eggplant isn't bitter, and doesn't need the pre-cook salting—now, lots of new bitterless varieties have been developed worldwide, too—but it does respond well to olive oil, salt and pepper, and a smoking hot oven.

Some relationships require a lot more work than others. In the case of eggplant, it was simply matter of finding the right one, which just happened to be French.

ROASTED VEGGIE MELT

MAKES 4

2 medium eggplants, sliced into ¼-inch/6 mm rounds
olive oil
2 large red bell peppers
1 (4.4 ounce/125 gram) ball of fresh mozzarella
4 large slices of country bread
4 fresh basil leaves, roughly torn
Basil Oil (p.97)

1. Preheat your broiler. Put the eggplant pieces on cookie sheets lightly coated with olive oil (eggplant likes to stick), and then brush some olive oil on both sides of the eggplant pieces (I use about 1 teaspoon of olive oil per piece). Pop the eggplant into the oven and watch it carefully, and after 10 minutes or so, when the pieces brown, pull them out, flip them over, and cook the other side. Remove from the oven and let cool.

2. To roast the red bell peppers, simply put them on a foil- or parchment-lined baking sheet (no oil needed), and make a few slits in each pepper with a sharp knife—this will keep them from exploding. Keep an eye on them, and when the peppers' skin blackens, flip over to the next side, and repeat until all sides are charred. Then, put your peppers into a bowl of ice water for about 10 minutes, let the skins loosen, and you can peel them off easily. Seed the peppers, cutting away the membranes, and cut into fat strips.

3. Make your tartines. If the oven's still on broil, you're ready to go; if not, preheat the broiler. Pop 4 large slices of country-style bread into your toaster, and once they're toasted, lay them out on a cookie sheet. Fan four eggplant slices on each piece of toasted bread, and add strips of roasted red bell pepper. Tear off pieces of mozzarella and place on top. Slide into the oven and let cook until the cheese melts. Remove, and sprinkle with a few torn pieces of basil and some Basil Oil.

JALAPEÑO PIMENTO CHEESE TARTINES

Pimento cheese is a Southern thing. You won't find a church potluck in Texas without it.

It's always been my default snack.

Just ask my mom. High school, college, and even now, one of the first things I do when I walk in her door is walk straight to the kitchen. I grab a Dr. Pepper and the pimento cheese from the fridge and get a box of Wheat Thins from the pantry, and start sipping and dipping.

There are more than three hundred cheeses in France, but there's nothing like this killer Southern sandwich spread made from grated cheddar, mayo, and red peppers.

Mom makes her own. So do I—but I turn up the pepper quotient and the heat. I make a roasted red bell pepper mayo; then I add chopped fresh jalapeño if I can (a friend from Dallas brought me a sackful once and I kept them in the freezer for months); another hot pepper if I can't.

When I make this, I stuff it in the back corner of the fridge, behind the jars of Dijon mustard (smooth and grainy) and bread-and-butter pickles that I bring from home. If X reads this, I'm going to have to find another hiding place!

JALAPEÑO PIMENTO CHEESE TARTINES

MAKES 4 TARTINES

4 cups/240 grams of grated cheddar cheese

¼ of a small red onion, finely chopped

1 to 2 medium jalapeño peppers (with membranes and seeds included if you like it hot), finely chopped

1 roasted red bell pepper (jarred ones are OK), finely chopped

about 1 tablespoon of chopped fresh dill, plus a little more for serving

2 to 3 tablespoons of Roasted Red Bell Pepper Mayo (recipe follows)

sea salt and pepper

4 big slices of country bread, toasted

Gently mix together the grated cheese, chopped red onion, jalapeño, roasted red bell pepper, and dill in a medium bowl, along with the 2 to 3 tablespoons of roasted red pepper mayo, and a pinch of salt and pepper. Refrigerate for a couple of hours before eating—it's much better this way. Spread on each piece of your toasted bread, and sprinkle with a little more dill to make it pretty.

> ★ **COWGIRL TIP:** In the summertime, I like to add sliced tomatoes and bacon to this, too.
>
> ★ **DOUBLE-DUTY:** Try Jalapeño Pimento Cheese instead of regular cheese on your burgers.

ROASTED RED BELL PEPPER MAYO

MAKES ABOUT 1 CUP/240 ML

I started making my own mayo when I moved to France, where, unbelievably, the store-bought stuff is awful. You can skip this step, and simply blend the roasted red bell peppers with a good mayo, such as Hellmann's, but making your own takes less than five minutes and makes everything better.

1 egg yolk

1 whole egg

2 teaspoons of Dijon mustard

1 roasted red bell pepper (see p.185),
   or you may use jarred

the juice of ½ lemon (about 1 tablespoon)

sea salt and pepper

1 cup/240 ml of vegetable or olive oil

Put the egg yolk, egg, Dijon mustard, roasted red bell pepper, lemon juice, and a pinch of salt and pepper into your food processor and blend. While the motor's running, very slowly add the oil. Taste for seasonings.

GRILLED BRIE, PEAR, *and* PROSCIUTTO SANDWICHES

Lord knows I love grilled cheese sandwiches, the most satisfying comfort food ever, so when my group of enthusiastic eaters on Twitter, LetsLunch, suggested that we all post recipes for a grilled cheese dish one fall, I couldn't have been happier.

I never need an excuse to make grilled cheese sandwiches, but this got me thinking. I was up against some pretty tough competition. Not that I would ever look at our monthly virtual lunches as a *contest*, but Cheryl Tan, author of *A Tiger in the Kitchen,* and I started this little group one summer when we bonded over our mutual love of bacon. We decided to post recipes for our own version of BLTs one Friday, and she outdid us all with her lattice bacon layer. Who does that, weave bacon for a sandwich?

Cheryl Tan, that's who.

Months, years later, we just kept posting recipes around a theme or an ingredient, and our little group grew. It now stretches around the world, from Paris to Los Angeles and over to Australia, too.

So for our grilled cheese day, I wanted to make something with a French accent. Which is how I came up with the Grilled Brie, Pear, and Prosciutto Sandwich.

I used Brie de Meaux, the sweet and creamy, slightly nutty cow's milk cheese from the nearby town of Meaux, 50 kilometers east of Paris, where it's been made since the eighth century. Brie de Meaux is one of only two cheeses that can legally claim the name Brie in France.

It's often called the "king of cheeses." Maybe because King Louis XVI asked for a bit of Brie before his execution.

Cheese and guillotines. Isn't French history fun?

GRILLED BRIE, PEAR, AND PROSCIUTTO SANDWICHES

4 tablespoons of butter, melted

8 slices of country bread

4 (3-inch/7.5 cm) wedges of Brie cheese

4 ripe pears, cored, peeled, and sliced

8 thin slices of prosciutto

1. Brush some of the melted butter on one side of each slice of bread, and lay the bread slices on a plate or your prep area, butter-side down. Stay with me. There's a method to this madness.

2. Layer the ingredients, dividing evenly, onto 4 bread slices in this order: brie/pears/prosciutto. Add 1 wedge of Brie to each slice, top with one-quarter of the pear slices, and 2 slices of prosciutto. The idea is to keep the wet pears away from the bread, and by doing it this way, the brie and prosciutto will keep the bread dry. Go ahead and top each sandwich with the remaining slices of bread, butter-side up.

3. Get out your biggest skillet, put it on the stovetop, and turn the heat to medium. When it's warm, put as many sandwiches that'll fit (you may need to do this in batches, depending on the size of your bread) in the skillet, and press down with your spatula. You'll want to do this again, every now and then, while they cook. When the bread's brown and crispy, give the sandwiches a flip. Let them cook for a few more minutes—until the second side is browned, and the cheese has melted—and eat immediately.

ADOBO SALMON
SALAD TARTINES

It's inevitable. If you live in Paris, you get spoiled.

For example, I have three boulangeries within one block of our apartment. Three. And they all make a full range of baguettes and other breads, along with tarts filled with fruit, chocolate, or lemon cream; madeleines and tiny cakes, oversize *sablé* cookies; lacy thin *tuiles;* and meringues as big as a cast-iron skillet.

When I first moved here, I was so excited to have a boulangerie across the street that I couldn't stand it. I'd buy fresh croissants in the morning and a warm baguette *de tradition* every afternoon between 5 and 7, right when they were being pulled from the ovens. Then I discovered the place down the street, where the baguettes were much better, but 25 centimes more. X thought that was criminal; I didn't. After that, I tried the boulangerie on the circle. I didn't like their baguettes, but thought their *chouquettes* were the best. So now I frequent all three: *pains au chocolat* across the street, baguettes down the block, and *chouquettes* on the circle.

And I wouldn't call any of these the best in town. They are simply the best in my neighborhood.

See? Spoiled.

Salmon's another example. There are three different *poissonneries* in the neighborhood that I like; where I go depends on the day of the week, because one's at a Wednesday/Saturday market, another's at a Tuesday-to-Saturday market, and the other place has really unpredictable hours but the best fish, since the guy who runs the shop also catches the fish. In a pinch, there's the salmon at Picard, the all-frozen-foods store.

If I'm looking for smoked salmon, that's something else entirely.

Every now and then I'll end up with too much salmon, which is how I came up with this recipe. Of course, I had to run across town to Poilâne to get my favorite sourdough bread to heap it on, but that's another story.

ADOBO SALMON
SALAD TARTINES

MAKES 4 TARTINES

14 ounces/400 grams of salmon fillets

½ cup/120 ml of a dry white wine, such as
  Sauvignon Blanc or Chardonnay

½ cup/120 ml of water

2 or 3 sprigs of fresh flat-leaf parsley

1 small shallot, sliced

2 (3-inch/7.5 cm) pieces of lemon zest

10 peppercorns

a big pinch of sea salt

2 tablespoons of good mayonnaise, such as Hellmann's

2 tablespoons of Adobo Salsa (p.323)

2 tablespoons of minced green onion or shallot

a handful of fresh cilantro, chopped

about 1 tablespoon of freshly squeezed lemon juice

sea salt and pepper

1 baguette, cut in half, split, and toasted

1 medium avocado, sliced

about 1 tablespoon of fresh dill, chopped

lime wedges, for serving

1. Poach your salmon by putting the fillets in a saucepan with the wine, water, parsley, sliced shallot, lemon zest, peppercorns, and sea salt. Turn the heat to low and when it reaches a simmer, cover and set the timer for 3 minutes and test for doneness. It may take another minute or two. Remove the salmon from the pan, place in a large bowl, and let cool.

2. Using a fork, gently flake the salmon into large pieces, and add the mayo, Adobo Salsa, green onion, cilantro, lemon juice, and sea salt and pepper to taste. Refrigerate for 30 minutes. When ready to eat, just heap a couple of spoonfuls on each piece of toasted country bread, top with avocado slices, fresh dill, and serve with lime wedges.

WINTER
BLT TARTINES
OR "HOW I OUTSMART TOMATOES, PART II."

I can be terribly impatient, especially when it comes to something as important as tomato season. I wait. I anticipate. I think of all of the things I'll make with them when the time comes. I make lists.

Then—*enfin!*—they appear, the star of the weekly markets, the reason behind the long queues.

I'm lucky that Joël Thiébault, a fourth-generation vegetable farmer with a stand at President Wilson market in my neighborhood, carries an abundance of tomatoes when they're in season. And in the most beautiful heirloom varieties I've ever seen. Some have tiger stripes. Others are bright orange or lime green. My favorites look like tie-dye T-shirts, with swirls of orange, yellow, and red.

The season in Paris is short, from about mid-July to mid-September. Then, like the summer rock stars they are, after a brief sell-out show, tomatoes disappear. And always before I can make half of the things on my tomato list.

One winter day, surrounded by heaps of sub-par tomatoes at the grocery store, I realized what I wanted was a BLT. It made no sense. It was the wrong season. But I wanted a BLT and I wanted it right then.

I knew just what to do. I filled up my basket with the sad too-firm Romas, and took them home. I split them open, drizzled them with some oil and shoved them in the oven. I let them roast, slowly, overnight. And I woke up the next day to the sweetest winter tomatoes I'd ever tasted. And I had my Winter BLT.

Sometimes impatience is a good thing.

WINTER BLT TARTINES

MAKES 4 TARTINES

4 big slices of country bread, toasted
about 4 tablespoons of Arugula Pesto (recipe follows)
8 Oven-Roasted Tomato halves (recipe follows)
8 slices of bacon, cooked until crispy
4 small handfuls of arugula

For each tartine, just spread about 1 tablespoon of Arugula Pesto on each slice of toasted bread, then add 2 roasted tomato halves, 2 slices of bacon, and a small handful of arugula.

> ★ **SWAP IT:** You may make this with fresh sliced tomatoes when they're in season, too!

ARUGULA PESTO

MAKES ABOUT ⅓ CUP/75 ML

2 big handfuls of arugula
¼ cup/1 ounce/35 grams of toasted pine nuts
2 tablespoons of olive oil
about ¼ teaspoon of sea salt
1 teaspoon of lime juice
a pinch of cayenne pepper

Put everything into your food processor and pulse until combined. Taste and adjust seasonings.

> ★ **DOUBLE-DUTY:** This is also great stirred into pasta or smeared on crostini and served as an appetizer.

OVEN-ROASTED TOMATOES

I like to put these in the oven before I go to bed and let them roast overnight.

**6½ pounds/3 kilos of Roma tomatoes,
   halved and cored**

olive oil

sea salt and pepper

herbes de Provence

Preheat your oven to 200°F/100°C and put your tomato halves, insides-up, on 2 foil-lined cookie sheets. Drizzle with a good bit of olive oil, and then sprinkle with sea salt, pepper, and herbes de Provence. Pop into the oven and bake overnight, or for about 8 hours, until they're wrinkly and soft.

CHAPTER 6

Riding Side-Saddle: Veggies

Before there was an Eiffel Tower—even before Paris was Paris—there were markets here, places where farmers could bring whatever they'd grown and sell for the best price possible. In the fifth century, Paris was still a Gallo-Roman city known as Lutetia, on the island that's now known as the Ile de la Cité. People lived there, so naturally that's where the market was.

It's the same today. There's a market in every one of Paris' twenty arrondissements, and then some; more than seventy markets are scattered all over the city. Some are covered, and open most every day while others are open-air, setting up and tearing themselves down twice a week.

I like the open-air markets the best, and I go to two of them each week; Tuesdays and Fridays are Belleville, after yoga; and Wednesdays and Saturdays are President Wilson. I love market days so much that I mark them on my calendar with a highlighter. I make lists for each one. I think I'll find one thing, but end up buying another.

What's available at the weekly markets determines what I'll make that week, and not the other way around. Instead of letting recipes dictate what I'll make, I let the ingredients lead the way.

The weekly markets are my guide to what's in season right now, this week, this particular day. Next week might not be the same. It's always changing. You never know what you're going to see.

Each market has its own personality that reflects the neighborhood it's in.

With barrels of olives, couscous, fresh dates, and men carrying oversize aluminum teapots filled with mint tea, Belleville's like stepping into North Africa. Chaotic and noisy, with men selling pineapples, shouting a sing-songy, "*Un euro, ananas, un euro, ananas*," it's a big messy scene, packed with people from the neighborhood, women wearing jilbabs, and lots of older men, waddling more than walking, usually with a cane in one hand, or a wheely cart in tow. There is much wheeling and dealing here. Slices of orange, melon, or nectarine are offered on the ends sharp knives for a taste. Haggling over prices is part of the fun; if you don't make a fuss, you don't earn their respect.

I try to get there early, but Belleville is always packed by 8:30 a.m. I go for the prettiest, cheapest sweet potatoes in Paris; habañero peppers and okra from a man from the French island of Antilles; Moroccan peppers; one-kilo sacks of black-eyed peas and black beans; almonds, cashews, and pistachios; and saltless peanut butter in a can. I buy fresh thyme, rosemary, cilantro, and dill for 30 centimes a bundle, and basics like celery, onions, and garlic for a fraction of what I'd pay in my neighborhood. I often buy so much I can barely carry it home.

At President Wilson market, the vendors are usually still setting up at 8:30, a good hour earlier than the crowds of well-groomed men in crisp shirts and slacks and women in teetering high heels with far too many small dogs in tow. It's not far from where I live, and I either walk or take the #82 bus to Place d'Iena. I start at the top of the market near the statue of George Washington riding his horse into battle and end twenty minutes later two long blocks away across the street from a brasserie with a postcard view of the Eiffel Tower and some very pricey coffee.

Despite its privileged airs, I love this market. There are beautiful flowers here and a foie gras man. Three boulangers, (one that makes rectangular-shaped baguettes), and three different *poissonniers*. There's a stand that justsells sea salt; another that sells only mushrooms and potatoes. I come to see the farmers, who peddle what they grow themselves right outside of Paris. You know them by the signs that say *"Producteur's."* And by the long lines. This is where I find Swiss chard in red, yellow, and white; cauliflower in purple and gold; and yellow squash for my grandmother's soufflé (p.233). Paris' Michelin-starred chefs come for Joël Thiébault's veggies. So do I. The potatoes still have dirt clinging to their skin, the lettuce with nary a brown spot on their leaves, and the carrots come with their bushy green tops attached. It's the sort of market where you can say to the mushroom seller, as I've done before, "I'm making roast duck pizzas. What sort of mushrooms do you think I should buy?" And she'll ask how many people you're feeding and fill up a brown paper sack with just the right amount. This is also where I buy fresh eggs and goat cheese every week from my friend Sandy, an Irishman who lives in Normandy. We always go for a coffee together. If he's busy, I'll stand behind the counter until he can take a break, and usually end up waiting on customers, along with him.

After I've shopped, bought and sold some cheese, and had coffee with Sandy, I'll sometimes stop by the crêpe stand in the middle of the market. Owned by a couple from Brittany, it's the place to get a hot-off-the-griddle Nutella-filled crêpe—the perfect hand warmer for the four-block walk home on a cold day.

CAULIFLOWER GALETTES *with* CHIPOTLE CRÈME FRAÎCHE

It was no secret that X didn't like cauliflower. He'd tell me every time he walked in the door and smelled it roasting in the oven, which it often was, especially when it was on sale for just 1 euro a head. He'd make a face, turn around, and leave the kitchen in disgust. Just more roasted cauliflower for me, I figured.

But even I can only eat so much. So one afternoon, when I had a whole bunch of leftover already-roasted cauliflower in the fridge, and no ideas for dinner, I decided to hide the cauliflower in something X might actually like.

I grated some sharp English cheddar (always a good start), chopped a few green onions, and threw all of it into a cornmeal batter, so these galettes would be more Southern than Gallic. I fried them and served them with a bit of chipotle-spiked crème fraîche on top.

The verdict? The next day, I came home and found X standing in the kitchen eating—not the chocolate chip cookies I'd made the day before but the few leftover cauliflower galettes, straight from the fridge, cold.

CAULIFLOWER GALETTES WITH CHIPOTLE CRÈME FRAÎCHE

MAKES ABOUT A DOZEN (2½-INCH/6 CM) GALETTES

1 medium head of cauliflower, cut into florets
olive oil
sea salt and pepper
1 cup/145 grams of cornmeal
2 teaspoons of baking powder
1 teaspoon of sea salt
½ teaspoon of cayenne pepper
½ teaspoon of cumin
2 eggs
1 (5.29 ounce/150 gram) container of Greek yogurt
1 cup//240 ml of water
4 green onions, sliced
1 cup/60 grams of grated cheddar cheese
4 tablespoons of vegetable oil
Chipotle Crème Fraîche (recipe follows)

1. Preheat your broiler and line a cookie sheet with foil. Position a rack in the middle of the oven.

2. Toss the cauliflower florets on the foil-lined cookie sheet, add a little olive oil, and salt and pepper. Toss it all together with your hands, then slide the pan into the oven. The florets will begin to brown after about 10 minutes—when they do, pull them out of the oven and turn them over, so the other side browns, too. This'll take about 10 more minutes. When browned on both sides, remove from the oven and let cool.

2. To make the galettes, in a medium bowl, whisk together the cornmeal, baking powder, sea salt, cayenne pepper, and cumin.

3. In a separate bowl, whisk together the eggs, yogurt, and water. Add this

mixture to the dry ingredients and stir together. If the batter is too thick, just add a bit more water. Gently fold in the cauliflower florets, grated cheddar, and green onions, reserving about 2 tablespoons of green onions for garnish.

4. Heat 2 tablespoons of the vegetable oil in a skillet and turn the heat to medium-low. When it's hot, spoon about 2 tablespoons of the batter for each galette into the skillet, fitting in as many as you can. You'll need to work in batches. Cook the galettes for 3 to 4 minutes, or until the bottoms are brown, and flip to the other side for another few minutes. You don't want these to cook too fast, or they'll be wet in the middle. Repeat with the remaining vegetable oil and batter. Serve immediately with Chipotle Crème Fraîche, and sprinkle some chopped onions on top.

★ **ADVANCE PLANNING:** Roast your cauliflower ahead of time, so all you have to do is assemble and cook them up.

★ **COWGIRL TIP:** Reheat your leftover galettes the next day—just pop them in the toaster.

★ **SWAP IT:** Try using grated zucchini instead of cauliflower.

CHIPOTLE CRÈME FRAÎCHE

MAKES 2 CUPS/ 480 ML

16 ounces/480 ml of crème fraîche or sour cream
2 to 3 canned chipotle chiles in adobo sauce

Toss your chipotles in a food processor to finely chop them up, or do this by hand. Add your crème fraîche or sour cream, and stir it up. Voila!

CHERRY TOMATO GRATIN

Daddy didn't have a big garden, but what he grew proliferated in what we called our very back yard (the "very back" for short), because it was its own fenced-in space between our regular backyard and the alley.

My dad was an adventurous gardener. One year he tried to grow watermelon. Another year, he planted asparagus, delicate French carrots, and Japanese eggplant. He always sowed corn ("High as an elephant's eye," he told me when I asked him how his corn was growing one year); jalapeños and cucumbers, which he'd pickle and send home with me in jars; okra and yellow squash; and fat tomatoes called Big Boy. There was always an aggressive gang of cherry tomatoes threatening to take over the back half of his plot.

When I'd come by, he loved to give me a tour of the garden. We'd tip-toe through the rows, bending down to more closely inspect the radishes that were nearly ready to be pulled from the dirt, or the green bell peppers that were beginning to turn red.

We'd always end up at the highlight: the cherry tomatoes. Daddy and I would pluck them from the vine, and eat them like bonbons they were so sweet. Hot from roasting in the Texas summer sun, with skins so tight that they'd pop when you bit into them, those tiny tomatoes were one of the best things about summer.

In the summertime in Paris, when tomatoes are at their peak, every now and then I'll taste a cherry tomato at the market that's nearly worthy of my dad's, and I'll bring some home and make this.

CHERRY TOMATO GRATIN

MAKES 4 SERVINGS

about 2 tablespoons of olive oil
1 pint/500 grams of cherry tomatoes, halved
1 cup/70 grams of plain breadcrumbs
¼ cup/13 grams of grated Parmesan cheese
2 teaspoons of herbes de Provence
sea salt and pepper

1. Preheat your oven to 400°F/200°C and drizzle about 1 tablespoon of olive oil onto the bottom of an 8 x 11-inch/20 x 28 cm baking dish.

2. Whisk together the breadcrumbs, Parmesan, herbes de Provence, and a big pinch of sea salt and pepper.

3. Stuff your little tomato halves, insides-up, as tightly as you can into the dish—there will be shrinkage—and sprinkle with the breadcrumb topping. Slide into the oven and bake for 30 minutes, or until the top is brown and crispy.

★ **COWGIRL TIP:** No herbes de Provence in your cupboard? Use Italian seasoning instead—it often has a similar herb mixture.

★ **GREAT WITH:** Roasted Salmon with Kalamata Olive-Basil Salsa (p.269). Pistachio-Crusted Lamb Chops with Cowgirl Chimichurri (p.252) or Basque-Style Fish en Papillote (p.271).

MOM'S BLACK-EYED PEAS *and* JALAPEÑO CORNBREAD

I can't remember where I bought my first sack of black-eyed peas in Paris. It was either at one of the North African stores in Belleville, or at the Filipino grocer in my neighborhood, and when I found them in a hefty 1-kilo bag, I felt like I'd just found a piece of home.

I made big pots of black-eyed peas and served them to X with jalapeño cornbread, neither of which he'd ever tasted before. It was dinner for him, and medicine for me—an attempt to ease the bad bouts of homesickness that I'd sometimes catch like a bad summer cold and have a hard time getting rid of, no matter what I did.

The black-eyed peas and spicy, cheesy cornbread were like a long phone call to my mom, comforting and familiar.

Whenever I visit my mom in Texas, she still makes this for me. She always worries about whether the cornbread's crusty enough, or cooked enough, or if she's put enough jalapeños in the batter. Of course, it's always just as it's always been—perfect.

X calls my cornbread *gâteau* and eats the triangle wedges from the cast-iron skillet with a knife and fork. He doesn't really understand the significance of this simple Southern meal, but that's okay. It's not for him, anyway.

MOM'S BLACK-EYED PEAS

MAKES 6 TO 8 SERVINGS

olive oil

1 onion, diced

2 cloves of garlic, minced

½ of a red bell pepper, diced

½ of a green bell pepper, diced

about 8 ounces/220 grams of ham (I like
   smoked ham, but you may use whatever
   ham you like), cut into fat pieces

1 pound/500 grams of driedblack-eyed peas,
   soaked for 8 hours or overnight

about 6 cups/1.4 liters of water

a big pinch of cayenne pepper

a few drops of Tabasco sauce

sea salt and pepper

Drizzle a little olive oil in the bottom of a deep, large stockpot, add the
onions and garlic, and turn the heat to medium. Cook until the onions
become translucent, just a few minutes. Add the red and green bell pepper,
and let them cook for a minute or two. Now, toss in your ham, drained and
rinsed black-eyed peas, water, cayenne, and Tabasco. I also add a pinch of
black pepper at this point, but not the salt—I add this later. Let this come to
a boil, then reduce the heat to a simmer and cook for 2 hours, or until the
peas have that nice, perfect "bite"—a pop of the skin, with soft insides.

> ★ **COWGIRL TIP:** There are two camps—the salt-when-cooking and
> the salt-later group, but I always salt all of my beans and peas at the end.
> It's how my mom always did it, and it works for me.
>
> ★**ADVANCE PLANNING:** Like many other peas and beans, black-
> eyed peas are better the next day, so plan accordingly.

JALAPEÑO CORNBREAD

4 tablespoons of bacon grease or butter

1½ cups/225 grams of cornmeal

½ cup/70 grams of flour

1 teaspoon of baking soda

1 teaspoon of baking powder

1 teaspoon of sea salt

1½ cups/360 ml of milk

2 eggs, lightly beaten

1 onion, diced

2 cloves of garlic, minced

1 cup/150 grams of canned corn,
   drained and rinsed

3 to 4 pickled jalapeños, chopped

2 cups/130 grams of grated cheddar cheese

1. Preheat your oven to 400°F/200°C and when it's hot, put the bacon grease or butter in your cast-iron skillet and slide it on in.

2. Mix together your cornmeal, flour, baking powder, baking soda, and salt. Now add your milk and eggs and stir this all up. Fold in everything else— onion, garlic, corn, chopped jalapeños and grated cheese, and then pull the skillet from the oven, pour the hot bacon grease or butter into the batter, quickly mix it up, and pour the mixture into the skillet. This is how you get that nice crispy brown crust. Pop this back into the oven for 40 to 45 minutes. It's done when the cornbread is brown and the top feels nice and firm.

★ **DOUBLE-DUTY:** Cut up your leftover cornbread into bite-size chunks, then toss onto a cookie sheet and slide into a 400°F/200°C oven for about 15 minutes, and you've got croutons—for salads, soups, or just snacking.

ROASTED OKRA *and* TOMATOES

My mom always got out her biggest cast-iron skillet for frying okra in the summertime. She made it simply, with a cornmeal crust. She never used a batter, which she and I agreed was a ridiculous thing to do to okra. Okra is not a corny dog, for goodness' sake. Mom's cornmeal way made crunchy brown okra nuggets, which she'd lay out on paper towels on a plate on the kitchen counter, and then cover with another layer or two, as much to hide them, I now believe, as to soak up the extra bacon fat.

When Mom wasn't looking, I'd sneak over and lift the paper towel and grab a few, then a few more. It never seemed like there was enough. I could eat a whole skillet's worth of fried okra.

Then I tried roasting okra and felt the same way. Sometimes called *le gombo* in France (derived from a Bantu word, and the origin of the Creole/Cajun word for *gumbo*), okra can be off-putting for its sliminess. Roasting it makes it nice and crispy. You'll be tempted to eat it right out of the pan before dinner's on the table, so do what I do—make a double batch.

ROASTED OKRA
AND TOMATOES

MAKES 4 SERVINGS

1 pound/500 grams of okra
olive oil
sea salt and pepper
a small handful of cherry tomatoes, sliced in half
Lime-Cilantro Oil (p.135)

Preheat the broiler. Put your okra on a foil-lined cookie sheet, drizzle with a little olive oil, salt and pepper and toss. Slide into the oven and cook until the okra browns; this shouldn't take more than 15 minutes. Toss your crispy okra in a big bowl with the cherry tomatoes and a some Lime-Cilantro Oil and serve warm.

★ **GREAT WITH:** Basque-Style Fish en Papillote (p.272), Fried Chicken Bites with Cream Gravy (p.258), or Mexican Meatloaf (p.266).

MAPLE-WHIPPED SWEET POTATOES *with* COCOA NIBS

The first year I was in Paris, I found sweet potatoes at the little corner grocer that's open on Sundays for nearly four euros for a kilo—a ridiculously high price, which I paid nonetheless, because when you're homesick, you'll do just about anything to inch towards a cure. Now I can find them just about anywhere, because *les patates douces,* like American cupcakes and the Gap, are trendy. Puréed, gratinéed, or folded with egg whites into a soufflé, they're still good old Southern food to me.

We never ate sweet potatoes any other time than Thanksgiving. At our house they were made into a gooey marshmallow-topped side dish to go with the turkey. And that was that.

But I like sweet potatoes best without a lot of fuss: baked, then split and stuffed with a pat or two of salty butter. Or like this, with a little maple syrup, and for good measure—and because I met John Scharffenberger of Scharffenberger Chocolates one summer and he gave me a sack to try—a few cocoa nibs, the leftover bits of crushed cacao beans used in making chocolate.

I can't remember what made me think of adding cocoa nibs to sweet potatoes in the first place, but now I can't imagine them any other way. Crunchy with a slightly bitter chocolate flavor, the nibs make a wonderful jimmies-style sprinkle right before serving. But remember, this is not a dessert, people. It is a vegetable. It is good for you, and you just may want to emphasize this to the kids at the table, so they will not want to eat any.

MAPLE-WHIPPED SWEET POTATOES WITH COCOA NIBS

MAKES 4 SERVINGS

about 1½ pounds/680 grams of sweet potatoes,
  peeled and thickly sliced

sea salt

about 2 tablespoons of butter

¼ cup/60 ml of cream

about 3 tablespoons of maple syrup

a couple of tablespoons of cocoa nibs (see Cowgirl Tip)

1. Put your sweet potatoes in a big saucepan, cover with water, and add a big pinch of sea salt. Cover, and turn the heat to high. When it boils, reduce the heat to a simmer. Cook for 10 minutes or until you can easily pierce the potatoes with a fork, then drain off all of the water.

2. Toss the butter in with the sweet potatoes and smash them up with a hand potato masher. When the butter melts, add the cream, maple syrup, and a pinch of sea salt, and be sure to taste, because you may need more (or less) butter, or maple syrup, depending on the sweetness of your potatoes. Sprinkle the cocoa nibs on top and serve. Lovely!

★ **GREAT WITH:** Fried Chicken Bites with Cream Gravy (p.259), Mexican Meatloaf (p.266), or Toni's Lamb (p.239)

★ **COWGIRL TIP:** If you can't find cocoa nibs, just use mini chocolate chips—it's not exactly the same, but I doubt you'll get any complaints.

GREEN CHILE-
GOAT CHEESE
SMASHED POTATOES

New Mexico and I are sort of like those relationships you read about in *The New York Times* wedding pages. Neither of us was looking for the other, but there was an attraction from the start. A spark. It deepened and grew over time. Texas may be my home state, but New Mexico is my heart state.

I started covering New Mexico-based stories back in the early 1990s for *Newsweek* and *People*. For years, it seemed like I was driving to Dallas' Love Field once a month to make that one-hour-and-forty-five minute flight to Albuquerque. I covered wildfires in Los Alamos and took flamenco classes; I met weavers with their own flocks of sheep and searched out vintage cowboy boots at the flea market. I bought a book on hiking around Santa Fe and started crossing trails off my list. And every chance I got, I ate as much fresh roasted Hatch green chile as I could. I had it on tacos and flat enchiladas, on eggs for breakfast, and on pizzas, hamburgers, and even in scones. On my way to the airport to go back to Dallas, I'd always stop at a grocery store in Albuquerque to buy frozen Hatch chiles. I'd triple-wrap them in heavy-duty foil and hand-carry them on the plane home.

I have a friend in Albuquerque who once tried to engage in a debate with me about the superiority of the green chile over the jalapeño. He said jalapeños were all heat and no flavor. I said that he was wrong. It's not an either-or situation.

There's room in my pantry—and my life—for both. For Hatch and jalapeño. For Texas and New Mexico. And for France, too, which has neither, but makes up for its chile deficit in other ways.

GREEN CHILE-GOAT CHEESE SMASHED POTATOES

MAKES 4 SERVINGS

1½ pounds/680 grams red-skinned potatoes,
  cut into 3-inch/7.5 cm chunks

1 teaspoon of sea salt

3 tablespoons of butter

3 tablespoons of cream

3½ ounces/100 grams of goat cheese

½ of a (4.5-ounce/127 gram) can of chopped green chiles
sea salt and pepper

1. Put your potatoes into a big pot along with a pinch of sea salt, and cover them with water by 4 inches/10 cm. Put the lid on, and turn the heat to high. When the pot boils, reduce the heat to low, and set the timer for 10 minutes. When it buzzes, check to see if the potatoes are ready by puncturing them with a fork—the potatoes should be soft, but not mushy. If they're ready, take them off the heat and drain them. If not, give them a few more minutes, and keep testing until they're done.

2. After you've drained the water off of the potatoes, add the butter, and give it a stir with your big wooden spoon. Now, with the hand potato masher (or just use your wooden spoon), mash up the potatoes, so some of them are smashed and others are still in pieces—we're not going for a smooth purée. Stir in the cream, then oh so gently fold in the goat cheese and green chiles—so the goat cheese will be in bits throughout rather than completely incorporated. Serve warm.

★ **COWGIRL TIP:** If you're close to New Mexico or any other place where you can get fresh roasted Hatch green chiles, by all means, use them. And consider yourself very lucky.

★ **GREAT WITH:** Perfect Roast Chicken (p.265), Pistachio-Crusted Lamb Chops with Cowgirl Chimichurri (p.252), or Mexican Meatloaf (p.266)

FRENCH BISTRO
GREEN BEANS

I once met a New York journalist who spent the better part of her stay in Paris seeking out the best places to eat *haricots verts*, the slender French green bean that are a bistro and brasserie staple, which come cold, tossed in a light vinaigrette as often they do warm. She ordered an enormous plate of them for lunch at the posh Hôtel George V. She'd also eaten them the day before, for dinner. Just haricots verts.

I totally got it. For as long as I can remember, I've been green bean-obsessed, and they've always been a part of our family dinners. We always had green beans for any sort of holiday, but I liked them best with fried chicken, dipped into a mound of mashed potatoes covered in cream gravy (still do). My grandmother would come to visit and she'd sit in a chair in a corner in the kitchen, underneath the window, snapping off the ends of green beans, then breaking them into pieces of twos and threes. She'd do this all afternoon—by the grocery sackful.

Long and skinny, French green beans may be slenderized versions of their fat American cousins, but they're really not that different. They both squeak when you bite into them, and they both have the power to round out a memorable meal. If Texas green beans go well with a Mason jar of iced tea at the family kitchen table, haricots verts go just as nicely with a glass of *vin rouge* at a sidewalk café or a picnic on the beach.

FRENCH BISTRO GREEN BEANS

MAKES 4 SERVINGS

about 1 pound/500 grams green beans or
   haricots verts, stems removed

olive oil

1 shallot, finely chopped

sea salt and pepper

E-Z French Vinaigrette (p.126)

1. Put a large pot of salted water on to boil, and fill a large bowl with ice water and keep it nearby. When the water boils, add the green beans, and set the timer for 3 minutes, so they're just blanched, not cooked all the way. Pour the beans into a colander, give it a good shake, and then put the beans in the bowl of ice water. Drain the beans again.

2. Drizzle some olive oil in your biggest skillet and add the minced shallots. Cook them on medium-low for a few minutes, just until the shallots start to become translucent. Toss in the green beans, making sure to have just one layer of beans in the skillet, so they cook evenly, and let them go for about 15 minutes or so, or until they start to brown. Put the green beans in a large bowl, toss with half of the vinaigrette (adding more if you need to), and serve warm.

> ★ **GREAT WITH:** Fried Chicken Bites with Cream Gravy (p.259) or Easy Roast Chicken (p.264)
>
> ★ **DOUBLE-DUTY:** Add Rosemary Potatoes (p.225) to your French Bistro Green Beans and vinaigrette for a great picnic side.

STUFFED ZUCCHINI
(COURGETTES FARCIES)

One of the things I love about cooking in France is the enormous variety of cute little dishes to bake, roast, and serve things in. Maybe it's driven by the mini-me ovens and refrigerators here: if you make a lot of something you have to cook in batches, and if you have leftovers, there's no place to store them. Still, I suspect that there's a right-ramekin-for-the-job aesthetic that's hard-wired into these people.

Here, in the land of Le Creuset, every recipe seems to have its own baking dish. There are bowls specifically for onion soup. Shallow, scalloped-edge dishes that are best for crème brûlées. Enormous clay pots for cassoulet. Special molds for the upside-down apple pie, tarte Tatin, and another for the long, flat *langues-de-chat* (cat's tongue cookies). And so forth.

While it may be a well-contrived conspiracy by cookware manufacturers to keep cash registers ringing, Living here has taught me that there really is such a thing as the right cookware for one particular recipe. Would a madeleine be a madeleine in any other type of shape? I think not.

Luckily, there's another traditional way of serving things here that's much easier on the wallet. I'm talking about *legumes farcis,* or stuffed veggies. They're not only as cute as a little Staub cocotte, but you can also eat what they're served in, which you certainly wouldn't want to do with cast-iron.

My neighborhood butcher proudly displays already-stuffed red bell peppers and sells the stuffing for DIYers—veal, pork, or a mixture of the two—but I prefer to make up my own concoction.

I love the idea of stuffing veggies with veggies. I particularly like them stuffed with this meatless, cheesy mushroom mixture full of fresh herbs. They look great on a plate, and if there happen to be leftovers, they're already in their own edible containers.

STUFFED ZUCCHINI
(COURGETTES FARCIES)

3 tablespoons of olive oil

2 tablespoons of butter

1 pound/500 grams of mushrooms, diced (stems included)

sea salt and pepper

1 shallot, finely chopped

4 round (or regular) zucchini

about 2 tablespoons of diced red bell pepper

$^3/_4$ cup/20 grams of fresh breadcrumbs

$^1/_2$ cup/30 grams of freshly grated Parmesan
cheese, plus a bit more for the top

about 1 teaspoon of fresh thyme leaves

about 1 teaspoon of finely chopped fresh basil

about 1 teaspoon of finely chopped fresh chives

about 1 teaspoon of finely chopped fresh flat-leaf parsley

1. Preheat your oven to 375°F/190°C.

2. Put 1 tablespoon each of olive oil and butter into your largest skillet and turn the heat to medium. Once this melts and the skillet's hot, add as many mushrooms as you can without crowding them (leaving space around the mushrooms allows them to brown; otherwise they'll knock into each other, sweat too much, and become watery)—you'll probably need to do this in batches. Be sure to add a pinch of salt and pepper as you go. Once the mushrooms are cooked, put them in bowl to cool off, then wipe out your skillet with a paper towel.

3. If you're using round zucchini, simply slice off the tops; if you're using a regular, long zucchini, carefully slice off the top third (the long way), leaving the stem intact. Scoop out the flesh, and roughly chop this up.

Put your hollowed-out zucchinis on a foil-lined cookie sheet.

4. Drizzle another tablespoon of olive oil into your skillet, add the shallots, and turn the heat to medium-low. Let this cook just a few minutes, until the shallots are translucent, then add the chopped zucchini and red bell pepper. Stir until this is cooked through—the zucchini will be your guide, turning opaque—then put this in a separate bowl to cool.

5. Mix up your breadcrumbs, Parmesan, fresh herbs, and a big pinch of salt and pepper; then add the cooled mushrooms, zucchini, and red bell pepper. Stuff your zucchini, add a bit more grated Parmesan, and slide into the oven for 45 minutes or until the tops are brown and crispy. Serve right away.

★ **ADVANCE PLANNING:** Assemble the stuffed zucchini in the morning, and refrigerate until you're ready to bake them for dinners.

★ **GREAT WITH:** Roasted Salmon with Kalamata Olive-Basil Salsa (p.269), Gascon-Style Pork Chops with Pepper Honey (p.256), or Easy Roast Chicken (p.264).

★ **SWAP IT:** Don't stop at zucchini. Stuff your tomatoes, red bell peppers, eggplant, and anything else you can think of.

ROSEMARY POTATOES

If not for Antoine August Parmentier, for whom a metro stop is named in Paris, there would be no pommes frîtes, no pommes anything around here.

Parmentier, a French pharmacist whose daily diet of potatoes helped him survive prison camp during the Seven Years' War, returned to Paris with a mission—to clean up the potato's bad reputation as food fit only for hogs, thought to cause leprosy in humans. His one-man PR campaign worked, and just in time to feed the country's poor, who were on the brink of starvation. And a few years later, when the French Revolution brought famine along with freedom from monarchical rule, the potatoes that had been planted in the Jardin des Tuileries saved the day.

Now there are more than two hundred varieties. And with evocative names like Red Pontiac, Dolly, Sassy, Rodéo, and Colorado, it's no wonder I love French potatoes so.

ROSEMARY POTATOES

MAKES 6 TO 8 SERVINGS

2 pounds/1 kilo of red-skinned potatoes,
  cut into 1-inch/2.5 cm pieces
olive oil
about 2 teaspoons of chopped fresh or dried rosemary
sea salt and pepper

1. Preheat your oven to 400°F/200°C.

2. In a large bowl, mix up your potatoes with a drizzle of olive oil, rosemary, a big pinch of salt and pepper, and spread them out on 1 or 2 parchment-lined cookie sheets. Bake for 30 to 45 minutes, flipping the potatoes over to the other side about halfway through. Serve immediately.

★ **COWGIRL TIP:** Always make more of this than you need, so you can reheat and crisp them up the next day in a skillet with a bit of olive oil. They're great with a poached egg on top, mixed into an omelette or heaped on top of My Big Fat French Salad (p.80).

★ **GREAT WITH:** Pistachio-Crusted Lamb Chops with Cowgirl Chimichurri (p.252), Easy Roast Chicken (p.264), or Kalamata Olive Basil Salsa (p.268).

PAN-ROASTED BRUSSELS SPROUTS *with* HAZELNUTS

One night, I was having dinner at Frenchie, one of Paris' hottest (and, with just twenty-eight seats, smallest) bistros, working my way through my pork fillet, when I discovered something underneath, something I hadn't recognized at first. Tiny *choux de Bruxelles,* it turned out, that had been roasted until they were brown and caramelized. Fabulous.

Well, I couldn't get to the market fast enough to fill up my straw basket with those cute little cabbage heads. How had it taken me so long to come around to Brussels sprouts? I wondered. I loved all of its cousins: broccoli, cauliflower, cabbage, and bok choy. I felt so foolish for ignoring them all of these years.

After I got my sprouts home, I roasted them, just like Frenchie's chef, Gregory Marchand had. To make things really interesting, I threw in some bacon and toasted hazelnuts, because, in my book, there's nothing that bacon and hazelnuts don't improve.

PAN-ROASTED BRUSSELS SPROUTS WITH HAZELNUTS

MAKES 4 SERVINGS

a small handful of hazelnuts
1 pound/500 grams of Brussels sprouts, halved
4 slices of bacon, cooked and crumbled
sea salt and pepper
Hazelnut Vinaigrette (recipe follows)

1. Toast your hazelnuts by tossing them in a cast-iron skillet (you don't want to use nonstick) over low heat. This won't take long, so watch them carefully and shake the pan around every now and then, so all sides get toasted. When you can smell them, and see that the skins are starting to lift away, pour them into a clean dish towel laid out flat on the counter-top, and use the towel to rub the skins off. Don't worry if there are small bits of skin still stuck to some of the nuts; this is fine. After they've cooled off a bit, roughly chop them up.

2. Put a pot of salted water on to boil. When the water's boiling, drop in your Brussels sprouts, and set the timer for 1 minute. Remove them, and let them drain in a colander.

3. Heat up your cast-iron skillet again—but this time, on medium heat. When the skillet's hot—and without oil—place your Brussels sprouts, flat-side down, and cook until they're brown and roasted. Flip to the other side, and when both sides are roasted, put them in a bowl along with the hazelnuts and bacon. Salt and pepper your sprouts.

4. Drizzle with the Hazelnut Vinaigrette and toss. Serve immediately.

★ **SWAP IT:** Instead of hazelnuts, try toasted walnuts or pecans.

★ **GREAT WITH:** Gascon-Style Pork Chops with Pepper Honey (p. 256) or Easy Roast Chicken (p.264).

HAZELNUT VINAIGRETTE

MAKES $^1/_2$ CUP/120 ML

1 shallot, finely chopped

3 tablespoons of Champagne vinegar

1 teaspoon of Dijon mustard

sea salt and pepper

4 tablespoons of hazelnut oil

3 tablespoons of walnut oil

1 tablespoon of grapeseed oil

Put your chopped shallot, Champagne vinegar, mustard, and a big pinch of sea salt and pepper in an old jam jar and give it a shake. Let this rest for about 10 minutes, then add your oils and shake again. Taste for seasonings.

ROASTED
RATATOUILLE

There are two ratatouilles in my life and I didn't feel like I could mention one without the other. There's the one you watch, and the one you eat.

Ratatouille #1: The Kind You Watch

Not long after I moved to Paris, X and I went to see *Ratatouille*, the animated Disney movie about Remy, the country rat with dreams of learning to cook in a fancy French restaurant. This was long before I'd hatched any of my own Cowgirl Chef dreams, but I identified nonetheless with Remy, and especially his frustration with his brother Emile, who had a big appetite, but an undiscerning palate.

I fought the same battles with X, who had unknowingly become my chief food tester.

A few days after the movie, X bought me a "Ratatouille" coffee mug, which I began drinking my coffee out of each morning. Sometimes when I'd notice that the last slice of cake or the last few cookies had mysteriously disappeared, X would say, "I guess Emile was here again."

Ratatouille #2: The Kind You Eat

I used to make ratatouille the traditional French way, with all the veggies in a pot or a skillet stirred up together. I wanted to like it more than I actually did. It was just too mushy, and I really don't like mushy anything. After reading Alain Ducasse's cookbook, I tried chopping up everything really small. Also fine, but not great. Then, I finally got around to doing things the Cowgirl way: I roasted everything, and it was wonderful. Emile, I mean X, said it was the best he'd ever had, too.

ROASTED RATATOUILLE

MAKES 4 SERVINGS

1 eggplant, cut into ½-inch/12 mm rounds, then quartered

2 zucchini, cut into ½-inch/12 mm rounds, then quartered

1 red bell pepper, cut into ½-inch/12 mm pieces

1 onion, chopped into ½-inch/12 mm pieces

about 8 tablespoons of olive oil

sea salt and pepper

12 halves of Oven-Roasted Tomatoes (p.197), quartered

4 large basil leaves, roughly torn

1. Preheat your broiler and line 4 different cookie sheets—1 for each veggie, because they'll cook at slightly different times—with foil for easy cleanup. Position a rack in the middle of the oven.

2. Put your eggplant on 1 cookie sheet, and the zucchini, the red bell pepper, and the onions on their own cookie sheets, too. Drizzle some olive oil on both sides of your eggplant so it won't stick (eggplant loves to do this) along with a good sprinkle of salt and pepper. Now oil, salt, and pepper the other veggies and roast them one pan at a time. The eggplant will roast the quickest—usually about 10 minutes—so watch it carefully and flip the pieces over when the first side has lightly browned. Do the same with the zucchini and the red bell pepper pieces, making sure to evenly brown each side.

3. When you've roasted all of your veggies, let them cool slightly, then toss them in a bowl with the Oven-Roasted Tomatoes and torn pieces of basil, and serve immediately or refrigerate. This is also great at room temperature.

> ★ **COWGIRL TIP:** This recipe is very forgiving. If you like more eggplant, then use more eggplant. Double or triple this for a large group.

MY GRANDMOTHER'S YELLOW SQUASH SOUFFLÉ

My mom told me that her mother made this soufflé every summer when she was a teenager at Woodlawn High School in Birmingham, Alabama. "I just remember that I loved it, which was surprising because at the time I wasn't that crazy about yellow squash," she said.

There's nothing not to like about a soufflé that features the curvy, slender-necked yellow squash, and includes tons of grated cheddar cheese and crushed Ritz crackers.

My mom still makes it every summer, in the middle of the season, when there's so much squash you don't know what to do with it.

And now I make my own version. It is an easy mix-it-up-in-one-pot thing; I love to whip it together whenever I get my hands on yellow squash at the one stand in the one market that seems to be the only place in town to have it. Lovely, light, cheesy, and crunchy, this soufflé goes with just about anything, from barbecue to sliced tomatoes. It's a bit old-fashioned, but that's exactly why I like it.

MY GRANDMOTHER'S YELLOW SQUASH SOUFFLÉ

MAKES 8 SERVINGS

1 onion, sliced

3 to 4 medium yellow squash, sliced

2 cups/160 grams of crushed Ritz crackers

2 cups/4 ounces/130 grams of grated cheddar cheese

2 eggs

1 cup/240 ml of milk

sea salt and pepper

1. Preheat your oven to 350°F/175°C and grease an 8 x 8-inch/20 x 20 cm casserole dish.

2. Toss the onions and squash in a medium saucepan, and just barely cover the veggies with water. Cover, turn the heat to medium-high, and when it boils, turn the heat down to a simmer. Let this go for 10 to 15 minutes or until the veggies are tender. Drain off the water, leaving the veggies in the pot—this will be your mixing bowl.

3. Mix your grated cheese with the Ritz cracker crumbs, and scoop out 1½ cups/100 grams for the top and set aside.

4. In a small bowl, lightly beat the eggs with the milk.

5. Add the cheese and crushed crackers to the squash, stir this around with a wooden spoon, then add the milk, eggs, and a pinch of salt and pepper. Pour this into your casserole dish, sprinkle the rest of the cheese and Ritz cracker crumbs on top, and bake for 30 to 45 minutes, or until the soufflé is set. Serve warm.

> ★ **GREAT WITH:** Gascon-Style Pork Chops with Pepper Honey (p. 256). Mexican Meatloaf (p.266), or Fried Chicken Bites with Cream Gravy (p.258)

CHAPTER 7

From the Farm and Sea

People come to France and they say it changes them. Forever changes how they see food—how they relate to it, make it, eat it.

Julia Child. Dorie Greenspan. Alice Waters. Countless others.

It's true: Before you know it, you won't look at a chicken the same way, or a stick of salty butter, or a baguette, an egg, a potato, anything. You won't be able to see anything without thinking about where it came from, how it was raised or grown, who did the tending.

You shop and you get to know farmers, butchers, cheese makers, fishmongers. Knowing the producers— *les producteurs*—makes it personal.

Take chickens. Go to any butcher shop in Paris and you'll see a variety of chickens, heads and feet still attached and neatly curled to one side, so you can see what kind of bird it is. A chicken with a red head, one with yellow feathers, one with black feet—when you choose your chicken, you choose *your* chicken, not just any old headless industrial prepackaged bird in a grocery case. You may watch, like I do, as the butcher chops off the head and feet, and uses a blowtorch to burn off the last few remaining feathers. You take the chicken home, and you unwrap it. Then you do whatever you're going to do with it. It's a process, and by going through this process, you connect.

That's why I called this chapter "Farm and Sea," not "Beef, Chicken, Pork, and Fish."

If you live in France for any length of time, one of the most annoying things is the slow-pokey way many things are still done here. It is not an on-demand, right-now sort of place.

But this old-school mentality, of meeting people in person when an e-mail would certainly do, grows on you. In fact, it's what made me become more closely linked to, and more appreciative of, what I cook and what I eat.

I actually know the man I get my goat cheese from. Heck, I even know the goats. Sandy the goat cheese man hasn't hired an ad agency to design a slick logo for his cheese. And he'd laugh out loud if he heard me describe his products as "artisanal."

But Sandy, who raises his own goats and sheep and makes cheese from their milk by hand, is indeed an artisan. Just as the butcher and the fishmonger, and the bread maker and pastry chef are. There's nothing trendy about it. They're just doing things the same way things have always been done.

By hand, in person. There's next to no marketing about it. It's just an honest farm-to-market business, where customers get to know who's making, who's growing, what we're eating. The idea of knowing where your food comes from isn't anything new. But I had to move from a small town in Texas to a big city in France to experience it firsthand, to meet the people and make the connections, and I'm forever changed because of it.

TONI'S LAMB

It was on a press trip, those awful group events for travel writers that involve military-like schedules, required group breakfasts, and unrelenting itineraries, that I first met Toni De Coninck. I usually avoid press trips, but I couldn't say no to a first-class ticket to Madrid.

So there we were in Spain. He was a food and travel writer from Belgium, and over tapas and Tio Pepe and group bus rides to museums, we struck up a friendship. When it was over, we said our goodbyes and swapped e-mail addresses, and I figured he'd just fade away.

But he didn't. And I didn't either. We kept on writing, and calling (this was way before Skype). A year or two later, Toni came to visit me in Dallas, and a few years after that, I saw him in Brussels. He got married and had two kids, I met X and moved to Paris; along the way, we all had dinner together at Toni's house in Ghent. That's when he made this lamb. It was springtime, the perfect time for lamb. We also had the season's first asparagus, which he and I were both excited about.

I'm not sure if Toni knew then that braised lamb was my favorite dish or not, but it is just the sort of thing that he would figure out. When I asked him for the recipe, he sent me a note with a list of ingredients, including, "garlic, left in their jackets." I just loved that.

This one's for my sweet Tonissimo.

TONI'S LAMB

MAKES 4 TO 6 SERVINGS

sea salt and pepper

2 to 3 pounds/1 to 1½ kilos of lamb shoulder

olive oil

1 onion, sliced into half-moons

5 cloves of garlic, left in their jackets

1 cup/240 ml of a dry red wine, such as a
Pinot Noir (see Cowgirl Tip)

1 cup/240 ml of water

2 tablespoons of tomato paste

1 cinnamon stick

5 whole cloves

3 carrots, peeled and chopped into 3-inch/
7.5 cm fingers

5 red-skinned potatoes, chopped into 2-inch/
5 cm chunks

a handful of fresh flat-leaf parsley,
chopped, for serving

1. Preheat your oven to 300°F/150°C and position a rack in the lowest part
   of the oven.

2. Salt and pepper your lamb, put a little bit of olive oil in the bottom of a
   Dutch oven, and turn the heat to medium-high. When it's nice and hot,
   brown your lamb on the top, bottom, and all sides, turning the meat with
   your tongs. When you're finished, remove the lamb and let it rest on a
   plate.

3. Turn down your heat to medium-low. If there's still some oil in the bottom of the pot, go ahead and add your onions—if not, drizzle a tiny bit
   more—and let them cook just a few minutes, just until they begin to
   soften. Toss in the garlic. Now add your wine and water, and with a

wooden spoon, scrape all of the brown bits off the bottom—this is the key to making a merely good braise really great. Let this reduce by half—it'll just take about 5 minutes, stirring all the while—then you can add your tomato paste, cinnamon stick, and cloves. Put the lamb back into the pot, and scatter the carrots and potatoes all around.

4. Tear off a big piece of parchment paper and press it right down into your pot, directly onto the lamb, veggies, and the juices. Even though we're putting a tight lid on the pot before it goes into the oven, this helps push more of the moisture down back into the meat, which will make it even that much more tender. It'll also make the sauce more concentrated and yummy.

5. Cover your pot and slide it onto the lowest rack and set the timer for 15 minutes, so you can check back and see if it's simmering. If it is, great; if not, adjust the temperature. Let this cook for 2 to 2½ hours, checking every now and then, and pulling it out to flip the meat over. It's ready when it just takes the gentle push of a wooden spoon for the meat to fall apart. Let it cool in the pot, with the lid on, for a couple of hours. You can eat it right away, but I like to make this a day in advance, because it always tastes better the day after, so I usually just slide it into the fridge until the next day.

6. To warm up your lamb, preheat your oven to 350°F/175°C. Put the meat in a casserole with some of the juices, cover with foil, and let it warm through, for 30 to 45 minutes. Serve with chopped parsley and crusty bread on the side with the roasted garlic.

★ **COWGIRL TIP:** Pinot Noir wines have a subtle though intense, velvety, and long-lasting flavor and light tannins, making them the perfect match for lamb.

STEAK FRÎTES *with* ROQUEFORT SAUCE

The biggest problem with the beef in France? It's not Angus.

As a Texan, I was raised on Angus beef. Burgers, barbecue, steaks on the grill— all Angus. We had a second freezer in the garage just to store the tender bacon- wrapped filet mignon steaks my parents would order from a cattle rancher.

The biggest difference between beef at home and in France is that most beef in the U.S. is slaughtered at two to three years-old versus five to ten here, so French beef is naturally going to be tougher because it's older. The more this meat is cooked, the harder it is to chew. Which may be why the French prefer their steaks bloody rare.

X was tired of hearing me complain about the inferiority of French beef, so he took it upon himself to research some of the best places in Paris for *steak frites*.

One night, we went over to Le Petit Chavignol, a little family-run bistro in the 17th arrondissement. We sat outside and ordered a carafe of wine and steak frîtes with Roquefort sauce.

The steak and frîtes filled up the entire oval platter; the Roquefort sauce was in a little ceramic ramekin on the side. I cut off a piece and dunked it into the rich blue cheese sauce. When the owner, Bernard Roque-Bouges, came over to say hello, I told him that I was from Texas and that his beef was excellent. He told me it came from his brother's cattle ranch in the Languedoc region.

X and I soon became regulars, and one afternoon Bernard invited me into the kitchen and showed me how to make his Roquefort sauce. It is not low-cal, and it is not going to be on anyone's "healthy foods" list. But it is a damn fine sauce, and it'll put you right in the middle of a bistro in Paris, wherever you happen to be.

BISTRO-STYLE STEAK

MAKES 2 SERVINGS

2 (8-ounce/225 gram) New York strip steaks,
   about 1-inch/2.5 cm thick
sea salt and pepper
olive oil

1. Preheat your broiler and salt and pepper your steaks on both side.

2. Drizzle a bit—only a little—of olive oil in a cast-iron skillet, and turn the heat on medium-high. When the skillet's hot, sear your steaks on both sides, then slide the skillet into the oven for a total of 8 minutes — flipping the steak over after 4 minutes so it cooks evenly. Let the steaks rest, loosely covered with foil, for 5 minutes. Serve them on a plate heaped with frîtes, and the Roquefort sauce on the side.

ROQUEFORT SAUCE

MAKES ABOUT 1½ CUPS/360 ML

½ stick/60 grams of butter
2 shallots, finely chopped
2 tablespoons of a dry white wine, such as a
   Sauvignon Blanc or Chardonnay
2 tablespoons of water
1¾ cup/420 ml of sour cream or crème fraîche
5 ounces/150 grams of Roquefort cheese
sea salt and pepper
a pinch of freshly grated nutmeg

1. Warm your butter in a small saucepan over low heat and add the shallots. Let them cook for a few minutes, or just until they become translucent.

2. In another small saucepan, warm your wine and water over medium heat. Let this cook until it reduces by half—this will only take about 5 minutes.

3. Add the crème fraîche or sour cream and Roquefort to the saucepan with the butter and shallots, and whisk to incorporate. Add the reduced water and wine mixture and season with salt, pepper, and a tiny bit of nutmeg. Cook over low heat until the sauce coats the back of a spoon, about 15 minutes. Serve warm, in a little bowl, as a dipping sauce for your steak (and frîtes).

OVEN-ROASTED POMMES FRÎTES

MAKES 2 SERVINGS

½ pound/500 grams of starchy potatoes,
   such as Idaho, peeled
olive oil
sea salt and pepper

1. Preheat your oven to 450°F/230°C and line a cookie sheet with parchment paper.

2. Slice your potatoes into fat sticks (or skinny, depending on your preference), and give them a rinse under cold water—this'll help remove some of the starch — then put them in a bowl of fresh cold water with a big pinch of sea salt and let them soak for about 10 minutes.

3. Drain off the water and dry your potatoes by wrapping them up in a dish towel (or two if you need to). Make sure the potatoes are nice and dry before proceeding to the next step, because if they're not dry, the olive oil won't adhere.

4. Put your potatoes on the cookie sheet, drizzle with a bit of olive oil, some sea salt and pepper, and give them a good toss. Spread them out and make sure there's space between them, or they won't get crispy. Bake for about 45 minutes, or until the potatoes are browned on the edges. Serve immediately.

SALMON *with* LENTILS

Lentils in France are mostly a winter thing. I know that. But I became so smitten with the delicate, petite *lentilles du Puy* that I didn't see why I couldn't have them other times of the year. No one ever said that I couldn't.

Lentils that have the *du Puy* name are the most prized lentils in France. Like Roquefort, Champagne, and other French specialties, du Puy lentils are fiercely protected with their own A.O.C. status, or *Appellation d'origine contrôlée*. That means that only lentils grown in the legally defined geographic area around the Gallo-Roman town of Le-Puy-en-Velay in the Auvergne region in the middle of the country can claim the du Puy appellation.

These lentils have a clean, minerally, almost fruity flavor, which is due to the volcanic soil they're grown in. When they're properly cooked and you bite into them, there's a bit of a pop through the skin to the lentils' tender insides. The tiny green lentils called "French lentils" in the United States. are similar, but they're not quite the same. If you can find du Puy lentils, by all means, buy them. Seek them out.

I always have a box of these lentils in my cupboard, and I love them like a true *Parisienne*. As for proper and effortless scarf tying, I'm still working on that.

SALMON WITH LENTILS

MAKES 2 SERVINGS

*I love this dish best in the summer, served at room temperature,
but you may also eat this warm.*

½ cup/115 ml of a dry white wine, such as
  Sauvignon Blanc or Chardonnay

2 5-ounce/150 gram salmon fillets

2 pieces of lemon zest, each about 3 inches/7.5 cm long

1 teaspoon of peppercorns

a sprig of fresh basil, plus a few leaves for serving

sea salt

2 cups/470 grams of cooked French Lentils
  (recipe follows)

a handful of cherry tomatoes, halved

2 tablespoons of fresh goat cheese

a small handful of pine nuts, toasted

balsamic vinegar, for serving (optional)

1. Put your wine, ½ cup/ 115 ml of water, salmon, lemon zest, peppercorns, and basil sprig in a shallow skillet with a big pinch of sea salt. Turn the heat to medium and when it starts to simmer, cover and set the timer for 5 minutes. Check for doneness and if you need it to go a little bit more, just reset your timer for another couple of minutes—this really doesn't take long. When the salmon's cooked, remove it from the liquid then pop it in the fridge, let cool, until you're ready to eat.

2. To serve, get out a couple of soup bowls, and put about a cupful of cold or room temperature lentils in each one. Flake your salmon over the lentils, add the cherry tomatoes and 1 tablespoon of goat cheese to each bowl, tear up a few basil leaves, and sprinkle on the pine nuts. I usually add a little splash of balsamic vinegar too—it goes really nicely with the lentils.

FRENCH LENTILS

MAKES 6 TO 8 SERVINGS

olive oil

1 onion, diced

2 cloves of garlic, minced

2 carrots, diced

3 cups/720 ml of Save Your Scraps! Veggie
   Stock (p.114), or you may use store-bought

1 pound/500 g of lentils du Puy or
   small green lentils, rinsed

1 bay leaf

a couple of sprigs of fresh thyme

sea salt and pepper

1. Drizzle a bit of olive oil in a heavy stockpot, add the onions and garlic, and turn the heat to medium-low. Let this cook just until the onions become translucent, just a few minutes, then toss in your carrots. Stir them around and let them cook for a few minutes, too.

2. Add 4 cups/1 liter of water and your veggie stock along with the lentils, the bay leaf, thyme, and a big pinch of salt and pepper. Put the lid on and turn the heat up to medium. When it boils, turn the heat back down to a simmer and cook until the lentils are tender but not mushy, for about an hour. Taste for seasonings and serve hot, cold, or at room temperature.

PROVENÇAL
FISH STEW

I once spent an entire afternoon getting far too much sun with a friend of mine at the Pont du Gard, a Roman aqueduct that stretches over the Gard River. The spot on the river has no doubt been a great swimming hole and the bridge a perfect jumping point for teenage boys since the first century, back when the aqueduct was built.

We stayed in a tiny town not far from Uzès, where people still hang cloth sacks on their front doors, many of them painted Provençal blue, for the next day's baguette delivery.

Worn out from the sun, I sat on the balcony overlooking the clay tile rooftops and fields of sunflowers—yes, I realize how postcardy this sounds, but this *is* the south of France—and drank a cool glass of rosé while my friend warmed up leftover soup she'd made the day before. It was light. Summery. And filled with chunks of fresh white fish and shrimp.

Nothing like the heavy *soupes de poisson* I'd tasted before.

Back in Paris, I unpacked my bags, went to my neighborhood *poissonnerie,* bought some fish and shrimp, and created this recipe. Because even though it's just a few hours away on the high-speed TGV, I can't always get to Provence.

PROVENÇAL FISH STEW

MAKES 4 SERVINGS

Homemade Fish Stock

olive oil

fish trimmings, such as a couple of heads
  from mild white fish and shrimp shells

2 leeks, sliced

2 carrots, roughly chopped

2 stalks of celery, roughly chopped

2 cloves of garlic, peeled and cut in half

1 teaspoon of peppercorns

a small handful of fresh flat-leaf parsley

1 cup/240 ml of a dry white wine,
  such as Sauvignon Blanc or Chardonnay

1 (6-ounce/170 gram) can of tomato paste

sea salt and pepper

Fish Stew

olive oil

2 cloves of garlic, minced

Homemade Fish Stock (see recipe above)

about ¾ pound/340 grams of red-skinned
  potatoes, cut into 1-inch/2.5 cm pieces

2 large summer tomatoes,
  seeds removed and juices reserved

a pinch of cayenne pepper

sea salt and pepper

½ pound/225 grams of a medium-firm
  white fish, such as halibut or sea bass,
  cut into 1-inch/2.5 cm chunks

½ pound/225 grams of shelled, raw shrimp

½ pound/225 grams of mussels

a small handful of fresh flat-leaf parsley, chopped

1. Make your fish stock. Drizzle a little olive oil in your stockpot and turn the heat to medium. Toss in the shrimp shells (and fish heads, too, if you have them), and cook for about 5 minutes. Now add the onions, carrots, celery, garlic, and let cook for 5 more minutes. Add 6 cups/1.4 liters of water along with the peppercorns, parsley, and bay leaf, the wine, tomato paste, and a pinch of sea salt and pepper.

2. Bring this to a boil, skim the foam off the top, and reduce the heat to a simmer for an hour. Let this cool off a little, then strain your stock through a piece of cheesecloth placed over a mesh strainer. You should have about 4 cups/1 liter of stock, which is what you'll need to make the soup. At this point, you may refrigerate your stock and make the soup the next day—it'll just take 30 minutes—or go ahead to the next step.

3. To make the stew, put a bit of olive oil in your stockpot and turn the heat to medium. Add the minced garlic and let this cook for a couple of minutes, or until you can smell your garlic. Add 4 cups/1 liter of your fish stock and the potatoes, loosely cover, and let this go until the potatoes are cooked, about 15 to 20 minutes. While this is cooking, de-beard your mussels by simply wiping the edges, and pulling the beards off gently with a dish towel—don't rinse the mussels or put them in water, or they'll open up.

4. Tear up the tomatoes with your hands, and add this to the soup along with a pinch of cayenne. Taste, and adjust your seasonings.Now you can add your fish, shrimp, and mussels and turn the heat to low. Stand over this, stir frequently, and in just 2 minutes, the fish, shrimp, and mussels, should be cooked. Serve immediately in big bowls, with a bit of chopped parsley, hunks of crusty bread, and the rest of your white wine.

★ **COWGIRL TIP**: Call your fish shop ahead of time and ask if they can put aside some trimmings for your stock.

PISTACHIO-CRUSTED LAMB CHOPS *with* COWGIRL CHIMICHURRI

There's a Greek place that X and I go to sometimes, at the bottom of the 16ᵗʰ arrondissement not far from the Seine, where the walls are painted a bright sunny yellow—to remind the owners, I guess, of a place that's far less gray than Paris. It is not fancy. There's a stand-up counter for lunch and a separate dining room for sit-down eating at night, which is when we usually go.

I usually order the *kefte,* ground lamb that's mixed with Greek spices, shaped into a torpedo, then skewered and cooked on a grill. With *frites.* And a salad with enormous chunks of feta, the best kalamata olives I've found in Paris, and fat wedges of tomato with a sprinkle of dried oregano on top.

I have always loved lamb. I don't remember ever not loving lamb. The first time that I tasted it was at a Greek restaurant in Dallas. I was instantly hooked, and even during my vegetarian period, I still ate lamb. It was my very non-vegetarian dirty little secret.

Now the secret's out. I will eat lamb chops, lamb legs, lamb shoulders, lamb whatever-you-can-think-of. Braise it, grill it, throw it in the oven, I don't care. As long as it's lamb and not dressed-up mutton, you can slide the plate on over.

PISTACHIO-CRUSTED LAMB CHOPS WITH COWGIRL CHIMICHURRI

MAKES 4 SERVINGS

6 tablespoons/50 grams of pistachios,
   toasted and ground

2 tablespoons of homemade plain breadcrumbs*

¼ teaspoon of ground cinnamon

⅛ teaspoon of cumin

sea salt and pepper

8 lamb chops, nicely trimmed

olive oil

Cowgirl Chimichurri (recipe follows)

1. Mix up your pistachios, breadcrumbs, cinnamon, cumin, and salt and pepper in shallow bowl.

2. Take out the lamb chops, rub a little bit of olive oil all over them, and one by one, dredge them in the pistachio mixture, making sure to evenly coat both sides. Put the chops on a plate, cover with plastic wrap, and pop in the fridge for 3 to 4 hours or overnight.

3. When you're ready to cook the chops, take them out an hour ahead of time and let them come to room temperature so they'll cook evenly, and preheat your oven to 500°F/260°C.

4. Lay the chops out on a foil-lined cookie sheet (this will help save you time cleaning up), and slide into the oven and cook for 10 minutes or until a thermometer reads 130°F/55°C— this should give you a nice medium-rare chop. Remove the chops from the oven, loosely cover with foil, and let them rest for 5 minutes. Plate your chops, one flat, and the other leaning against it (fancy!), with a spoonful of Cowgirl Chimichurri on top.

* To make your own breadcrumbs: Simply put a few pieces of stale bread in a food processor and pulse until the crumbs are small and fine. Store in a plastic bag in your freezer.

> ★ **GREAT WITH:** Maple-Whipped Sweet Potatoes with Cocoa Nibs (p.215). Green Chile-Goat Cheese Smashed Potatoes (p.217), or My Grandmother's Yellow Squash Soufflé (p.233).

COWGIRL CHIMICHURRI
MAKES ABOUT ⅓ CUP/75 ML

2 tablespoons of chopped fresh cilantro
2 tablespoons of chopped fresh mint
1 tablespoon of chopped fresh flat-leaf parsley
1 tablespoon of finely chopped red onion
1 jalapeño, finely chopped
1 teaspoon of sugar
sea salt and pepper
1 tablespoon of red wine vinegar
3 tablespoons of olive oil

Put everything but the olive oil in a small bowl and stir it all together. Let this rest for 15 minutes or so, then add the oil.

> ★ **DOUBLE DUTY:** This chimichurri is great on just about anything that you can think of—on top of lamb or beef, and on salmon and other seafood, too.

GASCON-STYLE PORK CHOPS *with* PEPPER HONEY

Expats tend to seek each other out, and it's no different with Americans. Besides a common language, we've got the same frame of reference, and even though we may not know each other yet, we already have a shared history. We're from the States, and now we're here, in France, where we all struggle with the language, the culture, the overall Frenchness of it all.

I don't remember how Kate Hill, who grew up in Arizona and other places in the West, and I found each other. I just know that when I got her first e-mail to me that said, "Are you free for a chin wag tomorrow?" I liked her instantly.

Chin wag? I couldn't wait for her call.

As soon after our first two-hour chat as I could, I hopped on the TGV to visit Kate in Gascony, where she's taught cooking classes for the last twenty-five years and lives in an eighteenth-century farmhouse in the tiny hamlet of Camont, a few hours southeast of Bordeaux. She's one of the leaders of the artisanal butchery and charcuterie movement, and is on staff at the School of Artisan Food in the U.K.

The skies are big in Gascony, and the sun heats up far beyond what I'd ever experienced in Paris. It reminded me of Texas, I told her, and I began calling her Cowgirl Kate.

I pulled weeds in her garden, gathered eggs from the chickens, and I sat outside, underneath the vine-covered trellis, and shelled coco beans for dinner. She introduced me to the Gascon brandy, Armagnac. We sipped it together one night on her canal barge, the Julia Hoyt. Moored in the Garonne River, we drank, and ate *tourteau*, the crab-shaped cake made from goat's cheese.

The last day of my visit, Kate fired up her Gascon-style barbecue, a helmet-shaped wood-burning grill, and cooked the most tender pork chops I'd ever tasted. Drizzled with *miel de poivre*, or pepper honey, that she'd made a few days before, they were out of this world. The food was so good and we were having such fun that I missed my train and had to stay another night. I really hated that.

GASCON-STYLE PORK CHOPS WITH PEPPER HONEY

2 pork chops, each 1-inch/2.5 cm thick
Armagnac or a good bourbon
sea salt and pepper
a few sprigs of fresh thyme, leaves removed
Pepper Honey (recipe follows)

1. Get out your pork chops 1 hour before you want to cook them, so they'll be at room temperature. This is really important—from-the-fridge chops won't cook evenly.

2. Preheat your broiler, and lay your chops out on a cookie sheet lined with foil. Splash a little Armagnac or bourbon on both sides of the chops and rub it in.

3. When the oven's nice and hot, salt and pepper your chops, sprinkle some fresh thyme on top, and slide them in. Cook for 6 minutes, flip the chops over, and cook for 6 minutes more (for a medium chop). Put a piece of foil over the chops and let them rest for 5 minutes before serving. Sprinkle more fresh thyme, and drizzle some Pepper Honey over each chop and serve.

★ **GREAT WITH:** Pan-Roasted Brussels Sprouts with Hazelnuts (p.228) or My Grandmother's Yellow Squash Soufflé (p.233).

PEPPER HONEY
(MIEL DE POIVRE)
MAKES ABOUT 1¾ CUPS/420 ML

1 lemon
2 cups/400 grams of sugar
2 small handfuls of black peppercorns

1. With your vegetable peeler, zest your lemon and put the strips of rind aside. Juice your lemon.

2. Put ¾ cup/180 ml of water in a medium-size saucepan, add the peppercorns and bring this to a boil—it won't take long. Then, cook this for just 5 more minutes on low heat, then strain, reserving the peppercorns and the cooking liquid; you'll need it in the next step.

3. Put the dark-colored water back in your saucepan, then add the sugar, strips of lemon zest, and juice. Bring to a boil, stirring until the sugar is dissolved and the syrup is thick, about 5 minutes.

4. Now, add the peppercorns back to the syrup, and cook on low heat for a final 5 minutes.

5. Remove from the heat, pour into an old jam jar, and let cool.

★ **DOUBLE-DUTY:**

1. Stuff pears with a tablespoonful of goat's cheese, slide them into a 400°F/200°C oven for 15 to 20 minutes, and when you're ready to serve, drizzle some of this on top.

2. Spoon the Pepper Honey over slices of Manchego, brebis, or any other hard cheese for dessert.

3. Stir a spoonful of Pepper Honey into your tea.

FRIED CHICKEN BITES *with* CREAM GRAVY

In spite of my phobia of anything that might involve steam tables, soggy bacon, and lukewarm glasses of Champagne mixed with orange juice concentrate, there is one brunch I look forward to each year.

On Christmas Day, after all of the presents have been opened, and homemade cinnamon rolls have been eaten, my mom moves on to the day's main attraction, what we've all been waiting for, our very Southern brunch.

Mom ties on her red apron, scoots into the kitchen, and with two large electric skillets, she gets to work on the chicken, frying the breasts in one skillet and the legs and thighs in the other. The biscuits have already been cut out and lined up on extra-large cookie sheets, their tops buttered. The sausage casserole is already in the oven. The eggs, broken and in a bowl, ready to be scrambled. The grits, measured in a cup, next to a pot of water that'll soon boil. Cheese, grated, on the side.

When the chicken's finished frying, Mom scrapes and stirs around the brown bits on the bottom, until it's transformed into a milky-thick, peppery cream gravy, just like the one her mother made. When she finally takes off her apron, we all sit down, passing every plate, bowl, and biscuit-filled basket until we've all gotten plates that are far too full, as we soon will be.

I make this, a smaller bite-size version of what Mom cooks in her side-by-side skillets. I'll serve them for dinner, a Southern tapas party, or even for lunch. Something this good can't wait till Christmas.

FRIED CHICKEN BITES WITH CREAM GRAVY

MAKES ENOUGH FOR 4

1 pound/500 grams of skinless
  boneless chicken breasts (about 4)
1 cup/240 ml of buttermilk
2 cups/250 grams plus 2 tablespoons of flour
sea salt and pepper
a pinch of cayenne pepper
vegetable oil
2 cups/16 ounces/480 ml of milk

1. Cut the chicken breasts into 2-inch/5 cm pieces and toss them in a plastic bag. Pour in the buttermilk, and squish it all around to make sure all of the chicken is well coated. You may need a bit more buttermilk to submerge all of the chicken; if so, pour a bit more on. Don't be stingy. Put the plastic bag with the buttermilk and chicken in a bowl, and slide this into the fridge for 8 hours or overnight.

2. When you're ready to fry the chicken, before you do anything, take your chicken out 1 hour beforehand—cold chicken will not cook evenly, and it'll completely mess up your frying temperature, so make sure your chicken is at room temperature. Turn the oven on to 200°F/100°C, and layer some paper towels on your biggest cookie sheet and put a wire cooling rack on top of that, so the fried chicken will stay crisp.

3. Pour about ½ inch/12 mm of vegetable oil in a skillet or a deep stockpot (this is what I use, and although it's smaller, and I must work in batches, it reduces the amount of splattering). Turn the heat to medium-high, and clip your candy or deep-frying thermometer to the side of the pot, but don't let it touch the bottom, or it won't give an accurate reading. When the mercury reaches 350°F/175°C, you're ready.

4. Put your flour, a big pinch of salt and pepper, and cayenne pepper in a plastic bag and give it a good shake. Add a few chicken pieces, give them a good shake so they're well covered, then pull each piece out one by one and shake off the excess flour. Do this with all of the chicken pieces and lay them on a plate.

5. Fry the chicken a few pieces at a time, making sure not to crowd the pot and to turn the pieces over so they brown evenly. Keep the lid partially on, to keep splatters to a minimum. Because the pieces are small, this will only take about 4 to 5 minutes per batch. Once they're cooked, remove the chicken pieces, and put them on the rack over the cookie sheet and pop into your oven so they'll stay warm and crisp.

6. After you've fried all of your chicken, it's time to make the gravy. Pour all but about 2 tablespoons of oil out of the pot, making sure to leave the brown crunchy bits, and turn the heat down to low. Sprinkle the 2 table-spoons flour over the oil and stir constantly until it begins to turn a nutty brown color—you're making a roux. Once you've gotten the right color, keep stirring and slowly add the milk. Stir and stir until it thickens—it won't take more than 5 minutes or so—and you've got gravy. Serve on the side, and dip away.

BUCKWHEAT CRÊPES *with* HAM, GRUYÈRE, *and* EGG

(LA CRÊPE COMPLÈTE)

I remember my first, bought from a street vendor along the Seine, somewhere near Notre Dame. Stuffed with ham and melted Gruyère, hot off the griddle and wrapped in a too-thin white paper napkin.

On that inaugural trip and subsequent visits to France, crêpes became my go-to to-go comfort food, something familiar, something cheap, something you could walk around with and eat. When I returned to Texas, I started making them myself, with ham and cheese, just like the ones I had eaten in Paris. I found out later that I was making the wrong kind.

This is France, and there are rules.

There are crêpes and there are galettes. Crêpes are made with white flour and galettes are made with buckwheat flour. Crêpes are for sugary fillings, like Nutella, the sugary chestnut paste *crème de marrons*, and salty caramel sauce. Galettes tend to be for salty fillings, like ham and cheese. But to confuse matters, they are all known casually as crêpes, as in, "I'm in the mood for a crêpe." You wouldn't say galette, even though that's what you meant, and you'd never find a restaurant that specializes in galettes and crêpes calling itself a galetterie; it is always a crêperie. Got it?

X and I have been going to Crêperie Josselin in Montparnasse for as long as I can remember. Considered one of the best in Paris, it's owned by 68-year-old Marie-Therese Benuzzi, who has run the place since she opened it in 1969, and who still presides over the crêpe-making two nights a week.

Marie-Therese's famous crêpes and galettes are as thin and lacy as the Brittany lace curtains in the windows. One afternoon, she showed me how to make them. Into a large plastic pail that looked more suited for washing clothes, she added eggs and dumped containers of milk with one hand, and with the other, which she'd made into a fist, she stirred. By feel. No recipe. That, she told me, was how she got the right consistency.

Marie-Therese made a crêpe to demonstrate how it's supposed to be done. The batter must be spread quickly and with a light touch, or you'll get thick, lopsided crêpes, she said. (Unlike American pancakes, which are simply poured onto the griddle, crêpes need a little help.)

This crêpe, called *la crêpe complète*, (actually a galette since it's made with buckwheat flour), is one that you'll find at any crêperie in France. It's the most basic, and usually the most inexpensive crêpe on the menu. I love these best because they're so simple, and because they remind me of that first one. You always remember your first.

BUCKWHEAT CRÊPES WITH HAM, GRUYÈRE, AND EGG

SERVES 4 (MAKES ABOUT EIGHT 10-INCH/25 CM CRÊPES TOTAL)

2 cups /250 grams of buckwheat flour

2 tablespoons of flour

1 teaspoon of sea salt

1 egg, beaten

½ stick/55 grams of butter, melted,
   plus a little more melted butter for cooking the crêpes
about 2 cups/480 ml of milk

4 slices of ham

1 cup/65 grams of grated Gruyère or Emmental cheese

4 eggs

1. First, make your crêpes. Whisk together the buckwheat flour, regular flour, and sea salt. Now, add the beaten egg, 4 tablespoons of melted butter, and as much of the milk as you need to make a batter that's not too thick and not too runny—it should look and feel like a thin pancake batter. I usually use almost all of the milk to get the right consistency, saving about ¼ cup/60 ml to add in later, right before I cook these up. Cover with plastic wrap and let this rest for at least 4 hours before you make the crêpes—*très important!*—crêpe batter needs to rest before it can become tasty French pancakes.

2. When it's crêpe-making time, check your batter to make sure it's still the right consistency—it may have thickened up a little, so just add some milk to thin it out if you need to. Now, dip a paper towel into a little bit of the remaining melted butter, and spread it around on your largest nonstick skillet on so there's a thin, even coating all over. Turn the heat to medium, and when the skillet's nice and hot, add a couple of tablespoonfuls of crêpe batter and with a spatula, lightly spread the batter around as thin as you can—they have these very cute wooden T-shaped sticks for this very purpose in France, and you twirl the "T" around in a circle in the middle of the batter—but a spatula will work just fine. Crêpes cook much like American pancakes—when you see bubbles appear, you know that it's getting done, so flip the crêpe over when this happens. Cook on the other side for just about 30 seconds, and then repeat with the rest of the batter until it's all gone and you have a stack of freshly made crêpes on your kitchen counter. You can let these cool and put them in a plastic bag, as I often do, and put them in the fridge until you're ready for crêpes, or make some right away.

3. To make your ham and cheese crêpes, simply butter the skillet again with a little butter on a paper towel, and turn the heat to medium-low. Lay your already-cooked crêpe on its most cooked side down, so it'll get nice and crispy around the edges. Put one piece of ham in the middle, and a small handful of shredded cheese, and let this go for about 30 seconds, or until the cheese begins to melt. Now, the fun part—crack an egg directly onto the ham, and cover with a lid or bowl, so the egg will cook. Check this after about a minute, and see if the egg has begun to set; just keep peeking until it's done. With your spatula, just fold over the edges of your crêpe a little, and slide onto a plate. Repeat with the other 3 crêpes. Serve immediately.

EASY ROAST CHICKEN

With *le coq* as its national mascot, it's no surprise that the French are big on chicken.

Chickens, just like wine, are designated by color and the area they come from. They've got yellow chickens, *poulets jaunes*, so called because the chickens are raised on a corn diet, which turns their skin yellow. Black chickens, *poulets noirs*, which have black skin and black feet, and black feathers, too, before they're all plucked. There's even a chicken that comes in the colors of the French flag, the prized *poulet de Bresse*, with its red crown, white feathers, and blue feet. Organic and free-range, the A.O.C.-protected Bresse, from the Bresse region near Alsace, are the most expensive chickens you can find in France, costing as much as 17 euros a kilo.

King Henry IV, who promised every one of his subjects "a chicken in every pot," wouldn't be too pleased about such pricey *poulet*, but he'd probably be happy to know that France is the number-one producer of chicken in the EU, and that every person in France now eats an average of 24 kilograms (about 53 pounds) of chicken each year.

I try to do my part. More often than not, what I make is a simple roast chicken with a *poulet jaune* from Challans in the Loire region. My butcher says these are the juiciest and sweetest of the bunch, and they may well be. I'm still saving for a *poulet de Bresse*.

EASY ROAST CHICKEN

SERVES 4

1 (3-pound/1½ kilo) chicken
4 to 5 tablespoons of olive oil
sea salt and pepper
herbs de Provence
1 onion, cut into 8 wedges
1 lemon, cut into 8 wedges
a few sprigs of fresh thyme

1. Position a rack in the middle of the oven and preheat the oven to
   400°F/200°C.

2. Rub your chicken all over—and in the cavity, too—with olive oil and
   generously salt, pepper, and sprinkle with herbs de Provence. Stuff the
   pieces of the onion and lemon in the cavity, along with some of the
   thyme. Carefully reach under the skin covering the breast and slide in a
   few pieces of thyme where you can. Truss if you'd like, though this
   chicken will roast just fine if you don't. Put the chicken in your roasting
   pan and pop it in the oven, breast-side up, on the middle rack.

3. Cook the chicken for 20 minutes, then flip over to the other side for
   another 20, and back with the breast-side up for the final 20 minutes.
   (The rule for chicken is 20 minutes per pound, so if you've got a bigger
   chicken, give it the time that it needs.) The chicken's ready when the
   drumstick easily wiggles, the juices run clear, or a meat thermometer
   registers 180°F/85°C degrees when placed in the thigh. Take the chicken
   out of the oven and let it rest, covered with a foil tent, for 15 minutes
   before carving.

★ **GREAT WITH:** Rosemary Potatoes (p.225), or French Bistro
Green Beans (p.219).

TEX-MEX MEATLOAF

My quest to find a really great hamburger in Paris has been a flop. Good burgers just don't exist here.* The patty is usually small and thick as a hockey puck, and it's either far too dry or not cooked enough. Then there's the issue of the buns, which are dinner-roll size and even smaller than the burger itself. Either that or they're faux American-style white buns that are far too large for the patty, never buttered and cooked on the griddle, and almost always dry or stale.

I eventually gave up, and I asked myself what qualities I looked for in a good burger.

Texture. Juiciness. Great flavor. Three qualities that make a good burger *and* a great meatloaf.

I spent the better part of a week one year playing around with meatloaf recipes, using the ground beef in France. To no avail: Because the beef here's so lean, I always ended up with a dry loaf, no matter what I did.

Pork is another story. Our cow is their pig. The French love pork, and good pork is easy to find here. So I asked my butcher to grind up a mix of pork and beef, with enough pork fat to make it moist and tasty. I pulled out my grandmother's recipe and borrowed a few of her secret ingredients—grated carrot and oatmeal—to make the meatloaf go further (this was a Depression-era recipe). Then I Cowgirlified the whole thing and turned it into something that tastes like a cross between a burger, a bowl of chili, and a taco, the holy trinity of Texas.

Of course, it is not a hamburger. I know that. But there's something wonderfully homey about meatloaf that's hamburger-like, and until I can get back to Texas, that's good enough for me.

* To be fair to the French, burgers are an American thing. I'm sure they'd say the same about our attempts at creating some of their iconic dishes. Anybody remember the 1970's crêpe restaurant chain, The Magic Pan?

TEX-MEX MEATLOAF

MAKES 8 TO 10 SERVINGS

1 pound/500 grams of ground chuck (15%)

1 pound/500 grams of ground pork

½ cup/60 grams of oatmeal (quick)

1 carrot, grated

1 egg

2 cloves of garlic, minced

1 onion, chopped

3 jalapeños (fresh is best but in Paris,
   I use pickled), finely chopped

1½ tablespoons of chili powder

1 teaspoon of cumin

½ teaspoon of chipotle chile powder

2 heaping tablespoons of tomato paste

1 teaspoon of onion powder

1 teaspoon each of sea salt and pepper

1. Preheat your oven to 375°F/190°C.

2. Put everything in your biggest bowl and smoosh up all of the ingredients with your hands—it's the only way to do this. Shape this into a loaf, and fit it into a 10 x 4-inch/25 x 10 cm loaf pan. Slide into the oven and cook for 1 hour and 15 minutes, or until the internal temperature reads 160°F/70°C.

3. Take your meatloaf out of the oven, and cover loosely with a foil tent to cool for 10 to 15 minutes. Slice and eat while it's still warm—and be sure to save some for sandwiches tomorrow.

★ **GREAT WITH:** Green Chile-Goat Cheese Smashed Potatoes (p.217), Roasted Ratatouille (p.231), or Maple-Whipped Sweet Potatoes with Cocoa Nibs (p.215).

SALMON *with* KALAMATA OLIVE-BASIL SALSA

In France, it's not uncommon to be served a small terra-cotta dish filled with olives along with wooden toothpicks to spear them with, when you sit down at a bar for a pre-dinner drink. This always makes me happy, and even more so because X doesn't really like olives. Occasionally, he'll eat one or two of the green olives at the Spanish tapas place that we both like, but if they're mixed into food or if they're warm, he won't touch them.

It's hard to keep up. I, on the other hand, haven't met an olive I didn't like, and I like to toss them into or on top of anything I can think of, from pasta sauce and pizza to breads (Cheesy Rosemary-Olive Flatbread, p.50), salads (Sunday Tuna Salad, p.120), and this chunky, yet light salsa; it's sort of like a tapenade and a chimichurri rolled into one, with lots of herbs and chopped-up olives and just enough olive oil to hold it all together.

I've spooned this on top of salmon, but I can't think of anything it wouldn't go nicely with. Yummy on grilled steak, chicken, scallops or shrimp or other seafood and fish. *Quelle surprise* — the picky Frenchman loves it, too.

ROASTED SALMON WITH KALAMATA OLIVE-BASIL SALSA

MAKES 2 SERVINGS

1 shallot, finely chopped

a small handful of fresh basil, chopped

a few sprigs of fresh flat-leaf parsley, chopped

a small handful of pitted kalamata olives, chopped

1 tablespoon of capers, chopped

$\frac{1}{2}$ teaspoon of red pepper flakes

1 teaspoon of red wine vinegar

sea salt and pepper

4 tablespoons of olive oil, plus more for coating the salmon

2 5-ounce/150 gram salmon fillets, with skin

1. In an old jam jar, mix up your minced shallot, basil, parsley, olives, capers, red pepper flakes, red wine vinegar, and a pinch of salt and pepper. Let this rest for 10 minutes. Then add 4 tablespoons of olive oil, give it a shake, and let the mixture rest for a half-hour, at least, before serving—the longer this hangs out, the better it tastes.

2. Preheat your broiler. Rinse and pat dry the salmon, and rub about 1 tablespoon of olive oil on each, making sure to evenly coat (and include the skin). Place the salmon fillets on a parchment-lined cookie sheet, give them a little salt and pepper, and slide into the oven. Watch carefully—it'll only take about 5 to 7 minutes to cook, depending on the thickness of your salmon, and how you like your salmon cooked. When it's ready, remove from the oven and let it rest with a little foil tent on top for a few minutes. Serve your salmon with a spoonful of Kalamata Olive-Basil Salsa on top.

BASQUE-STYLE FISH EN PAPILLOTE

It had been snowing in Paris for weeks, and we needed to get away. So for Christmas, X, Rose, and I piled in the car and headed to the southwest. To Biarritz, a place that can be so cold in the summer that you've got to wear layers.

But we didn't care. We were ready to take our chances.

We drove for two days, mostly in the snow, but by the time we got to Biarritz, the temperatures were soaring, nearly 75 degrees. We ate lunch outside at a seaside café in St. Jean-de-Luz, without jackets. We ran with Rose on the beach.

For Christmas Eve dinner, I bought fresh fish in Biarritz at the market across from Bar Jean, our favorite *pintxos* bar (that's Basque for tapas). After we'd drunk some Champagne and eaten the traditional first course of foie gras on Pringles potato chips, I made this.

I love preparing fish this way because it's easy, quick, and it doesn't smell up the kitchen. The little parchment package keeps everything super-moist, but more important, it's fun to tear open the paper and see what's inside.

Which seemed fitting, being Christmas and all.

BASQUE-STYLE FISH EN PAPILLOTE

MAKES 2 SERVINGS

½ cup/120 ml of a dry white wine, such as
  Sauvignon Blanc or Chardonnay
½ cup/120 ml of water
6 sprigs of fresh thyme
2 6- to 8-ounce/150 gram sole or flounder fillets
about 5 ounces/45 grams of cured chorizo,
  thinly sliced 8 to 10 pieces per serving
sea salt and pepper
a pinch of piment d'Espelette or cayenne pepper

1. Preheat your oven to 450°F/230°C.

2. Put the wine, water, and 2 sprigs of thyme in a small saucepan over medium heat and let this reduce by half; it'll just take 5 to 10 minutes. Once it reduces, just turn off the heat and let this cool.

3. Tear off 2 pieces of parchment paper, a couple of times bigger than your fish, and lay them flat on a rimmed cookie sheet. You're going to fold the parchment over the fish like a book. Place a fillet on each one of the pieces of paper, layer some chorizo on top, then a couple of sprigs of thyme. Do the same with the other piece of fish. Pour half of the wine-water mixture on each fish. Now, with each one, fold over the paper, and starting at one corner, just fold and roll up the paper all the way around, and tuck the end under—it'll end up making a semi-circle.

4. Slide your fish into the oven for 10 minutes and serve, as is, on a plate. That way, everyone can tear into their own—that's the fun of it.

> ★ **COWGIRL TIP:** Both the Marine Stewardship Council and Monterey Bay Aquarium Seafood Watch are great sources for checking on sustainability of specific species of fish.

CHAPTER 8

Desserts

Nobody does desserts like the French. The soufflés, the mousses, the pastries. The mille feuilles, éclairs, macarons. The perfectly symmetrical tarts with paper-thin slices of pears fanned in a circle, raspberries lined up in neat rows. I still stop and stare in the windows of the pâtisseries and boulangeries.

Some of these things are easier to make than you think. Everyone here didn't go to pastry school. They learned how to make cakes and tarts from their moms, and their moms, before that.

Some observations: The French make cakes, but they're not like our big fluffy American multilayered ones covered with swirls of sugary icing. They don't ice their cakes at all; instead, they'll dust the top with a light sprinkle of powdered sugar. Most French dessert recipes call for separating the eggs, with the whites whipped and folded in at the end. Making a caramel sauce is something everyone seems to know how to do.

From my Easy-Bake Oven days to today, I've always loved making desserts, but when I first moved to France, everything I baked was a flop. The flour here is different. The butter's not the same. Recipes I could count on every single time back in the States didn't work anymore.

For a long time, I just wanted to make a cookie that didn't spread all over the pan.

It took awhile, but I finally figured out which flours worked best with which cookies—I use different flours for chocolate chip than I do for snickerdoodles— and which ones are better for cakes. After I was able to replicate my favorite American desserts, I started trying French recipes, too, ones that were more old-fashioned than chic. Rice pudding. French chocolate sauce. Cherry compote. Then I began mixing and matching, blending American ingredients with French techniques (Peanut Butter Soufflés, p.70), or simply combining the two to come up with something completely new (Slice & Bake Hazelnut-Chocolate Chip Cookies, p.66).

I've always had a sweet spot for desserts—making them and eating them, too. When I plan dinners, more often than not, I first try to imagine what I'll make for dessert, then I'll work my way backwards to the appetizers. When I eat out, it's the same thing. I always look at the dessert menu first, make my pick, and then decide about everything else.

I've heard about people who like to share dessert or can even skip dessert altogether. Other than an obligatory bite offered for a taste, I don't believe in sharing when it comes to desserts. And skipping? Well, that was just for school.

CHERRY COMPOTE

My first cherries came out of a jar and were plopped into a glass—decorations to be fished out of cocktails I was too young to drink.

We didn't have fresh cherries in Texas, not in the '70s. Once we got them, I became a big fan.

So naturally I sought them out when I moved to France. This much I've learned about cherries while living here: 1) The season is painfully short, and I never feel like I get to eat enough. 2) There are a dozen different varieties here, ranging from sour to sweet and in deep purplish reds to bright yellow. 3) Once you buy them, you'd better be ready to eat them. They go south quickly. 4) Pitting them is messy. My kitchen always looks like a crime scene afterward, with red splatters on the walls, cabinets, and floor. 5) They really do grow in pairs, like cute little cherry couples. 6) I love the sweet ones the best.

I also figured out that while cherries are just fine on their own and don't need any help in bringing out their flavor, they're probably one of the most mixable and matchable fruits around; they go with just about anything. They hold their own with savory dishes like duck breast or lamb, and they work just as nicely in a sweet pie.

Take this compote, infused with just a little bit of lemon and rosemary. I've paired this with cheese, and spooned it on ice cream. I've swirled it into yogurt and made it into its own little tart. I've thought about doing other things with it, too, but by the time I get around to it, the season's over and it's back to yearning.

CHERRY COMPOTE

MAKES 6 TO 8 SERVINGS

1 pound/500 grams of cherries, pitted

3 strips of lemon zest, each 2 inches/5 cm long

1 cinnamon stick

1 sprig of fresh rosemary

¼ cup/50 grams of sugar

Put everything in your saucepan with just enough water to cover the cherries—I usually use about 1 cup/240 ml—and cook over low heat for about 15 minutes, or until the cherries soften a very tiny bit (you don't want mushy cherries). Let them cool in the pan, remove the cinnamon stick and rosemary, and refrigerate.

★ **GREAT WITH:** your morning yogurt, or with Buttermilk Ice Cream (p.298), on top of Rice Pudding (p.286), Grilled Orange-Vanilla Pound Cake (p.308). Or use it as a filling for a Croustade (p.280).

GRILLED ORANGE-VANILLA POUND CAKE *with* STRAWBERRIES

In France, there's a cake that's available at just about every boulangerie called *quatre-quarts*, or "four-fourths." Four equal parts flour, butter, sugar, and eggs. Same as a pound cake.

But not the same.

I've baked both, and even though the ingredients are identical, the way you put them together is different. The French version separates the eggs and folds in the whites at the end (*quelle surprise*), whereas my mom's recipe uses sour cream as part of the butter, adds whole eggs one at a time, and you beat them for about a minute each. Guess which recipe made the fluffiest cake.

I always liked this cake best the first day while it was still warm. Once it cooled, so did my interest.

My mom started reheating pieces in the skillet with butter and serving them hot off the griddle, crispy around the edges and warm all the way through.

It might sound wrong to fry up slices of already buttery cake in butter, but if it is, I don't wanna be right.

GRILLED ORANGE-VANILLA POUND CAKE WITH STRAWBERRIES

MAKES 1 LOAF

Pound Cake

the zest of 1 orange

1½ cups/300 grams of sugar

1 stick/125 grams of butter, at room temperature

3 eggs, at room temperature

1½ cups/200 grams of flour

¼ teaspoon of baking soda

a pinch of sea salt

½ cup/115 grams of crème fraîche or sour cream

1 teaspoon of vanilla extract

Berries

1 pint/450 grams of strawberries, hulled and sliced

⅓ cup/65 grams of sugar (you may not need all of this; it depends on how sweet your berries are)

the zest of ½ lemon

butter

1. Make your cake. Line a 4¼ x 10-inch/11 x 25 cm loaf pan with parchment paper. You don't preheat your oven.

2. Toss the orange zest in a small bowl with your sugar, and rub it together with your fingers so the oil from the zest will help perfume the sugar.

3. Pour the orange sugar in your mixing bowl, and beat it with the softened butter until it's light yellow and fluffy. Add your eggs one at a time, beating for about 1 minute each—this will help make the cake airy and light, so don't rush this step.

4. Whisk together the flour, baking soda, and pinch of salt, and add half of this to the mixture. Now, add half of the crème fraîche or sour cream. Add the second half of the flour mixture, then the second half of the crème fraîche or sour cream, mixing well between each. Finally, add the vanilla. Pour the batter into your loaf pan and turn the oven to 325°F/160°C. Bake for an hour and a half, or until a toothpick or knife inserted in the middle of the cake comes out clean. Cool for 10 minutes on a rack before you lift the cake out of the pan.

5. To serve the cake, first, gently mix your strawberries with the sugar and the lemon zest and set aside. Cut your pound cake into thick, 1-inch/2.5 cm slices, and melt some butter in your skillet over medium-low heat. When the butter sizzles, add your cake and cook 'til it's brown and crispy on each side. Add a spoonful of strawberries and dig in. I like this for dessert as well as for breakfast, and afternoon coffee time, too.

★ **SWAP-IT:** Strawberries are just the beginning. You can put whatever berries or fruit you've got on top of this little cake, and add a drizzle of French Chocolate Sauce (p.296) or Salty Caramel Sauce (p.287), and maybe a scoop of Buttermilk Ice Cream (p.298), too.

HALF-BAKED
CHOCOLATE CAKES
(MOELLEUX AU CHOCOLAT)

Brownie-like on the outside with gooey warm insides—talk about a great idea. These cakes probably began as a mistake somewhere, someone with an oven not unlike mine, a rascal of an appliance that says one thing—I'm hot! I'm 375 degrees! I'm ready to bake!—and then does another. Cools down to 200°, then it's—Whoops! —up to 450°. Cakes and cookies on a roller coaster ride in there, not knowing what to do.

For a long time, I'd simply point at the words on the menu when I wanted to order the French cake with the impossible-to-pronounce name. MWHEY-luh, or, as X told me, slightly incorrect but easier, MWAH-luh. At some point it just became easier to make it myself than to suffer mispronouncing and being corrected in public, either by X or by a waiter (they love to do this, too).

Sold all over the place—in bistros, restaurants, and even Picard, the store that only sells frozen food—the cake that doesn't even bake all the way couldn't be hard to make, I figured. And it's not. The only trick is not letting it go too far. The cakes will lift up and you're looking for an ever-so-slight jiggle on the top. And that's all I'm going to say about that.

HALF-BAKED CHOCOLATE CAKES
(MOELLEUX AU CHOCOLAT)

MAKES 6 SERVINGS

2 sticks/250 grams of butter,
  plus more for buttering ramekins
12 ounces/310 grams of good quality
  semi-sweet chocolate (about 2 cups chopped)
5 eggs
¾ cup/160 grams of sugar
¾ cup/200 grams of flour
a pinch of sea salt
powdered sugar, for serving

1. Preheat your oven to 400°F/200°C, generously butter the insides of 6
½-cup (4-ounce) ramekins, and put them on a foil-lined cookie sheet.

2. Melt the butter and chocolate together in the top of a double boiler, stirring every now and then. When the butter and chocolate have melted,
remove from the heat, and let this cool down a little.

3. In your mixer, beat the eggs until they're light, for about 3 or 4 minutes.
Now toss in your sugar, flour, and a pinch of sea salt, and combine. Add
the cooled, melted chocolate and mix well—you're nearly there. Divide
the batter among the ramekins, and cook for 15 to 20 minutes, or until
the little cakes begin to slightly lift out. Gently turn the ramekins
upside-down onto dessert plates, and serve immediately, with a sprinkle
of powdered sugar on top.

★ **A NOTE ABOUT CHOCOLATE:** I use 66% Callebaut chocolate
pastilles in France, but plain old Baker's chocolate works just as well.

★ **ADVANCE PLANNING:** Assemble the cakes up to a day ahead
of time and keep them in the fridge until you're ready to bake.

RICE PUDDING *with* SALTY CARAMEL SAUCE

It had been years—decades probably—since I'd eaten rice pudding, and I can't say I'd *missed* it. But when I saw the café au lait bowl of rice pudding at L'Ami Jean, where Basque chef Stéphane Jego presides over the kitchen at what is still one of Paris' top bistros, I knew something was different. Fluffy, not heavy, and heaps of it, served with caramel whipped cream on the side and a wooden paddle so you could share. Share?

Whenever we'd go back, X would wax nostalgic about the *riz au lait* of his childhood. It was served in enormous bowls, and instead of caramel whipped cream on the side, it came with salty caramel sauce on top, which sounded even better.

I'd had salty caramel many times on trips to Brittany. Fleur de sel, sea salt hand-harvested off the Brittany coast, is the special ingredient in the heavily salted caramels that are a traditional treat in the region. And I'd ordered salty caramel sauce many times on top of dessert crêpes at Crêperie Josselin (see p.261). I asked Marie-Therese if she'd share her recipe with me and show me how to put it together, which she was happy to do.

This is an adaptation of her sauce, along with my rice pudding. Pour at your own risk.

RICE PUDDING WITH
SALTY CARAMEL SAUCE

MAKES 8 SERVINGS

4¾ cups/1.12 liters of milk

7 tablespoons/120 grams of sugar, divided

¾ cup/115 grams of Arborio or any
   other short-grain rice

½ teaspoon of sea salt

1 teaspoon of vanilla extract

1 cup/240 ml of cream

Salty Caramel Sauce (recipe follows)

1. Combine the milk, 5 tablespoons of sugar, rice, and sea salt in a heavy
   saucepan over medium-high heat, and bring this to a boil.

2. After this boils, reduce your heat to medium-low—just to a simmer—
   and cook until the rice is tender and the mixture is thick and porridge-
   like, but still has some liquid—the rice will continue to absorb the milk
   after it's cool. Stir every now and then. Just be patient—this will take 20
   to 35 minutes. When it's ready, remove from the heat, pour into a bowl,
   and add the vanilla. Let this cool before covering with plastic wrap, making sure to press the plastic down onto the top of the pudding, so you
   don't get "pudding skin." Then refrigerate for a few hours or until it's
   completely cool.

3. A half-hour before you want to serve the pudding , beat the cream and
   remaining 2 tablespoons of sugar together until medium peaks form.
   Fold this into the chilled pudding and refrigerate. Serve your rice pudding, Frenchy-style, in big bowls with warm caramel sauce on the side.

SALTY CARAMEL SAUCE

MAKES ABOUT 2 CUPS/480 ML

1½ cups/300 grams of sugar
¼ cup/60 ml of water
1 stick/125 grams of butter
¾ cup/180 ml of crème fraîche or sour cream
1 teaspoon of sea salt (see Cowgirl Tip)

1. Get out your heaviest, deepest pot (this will help reduce caramel splatters), and a long wooden spoon.

2. Put your sugar and water in the pot, give it a stir or two so it combines, and turn the heat to medium-high. Now, just leave it alone. It'll bubble continuously. Don't even think about stirring the pot. The less you mess with caramel, the better. After 10 to 15 minutes, you'll notice the sugar beginning to darken around the edges of the pot. I'll repeat: Don't stir. But you may, if you want to (and usually I do), pick up the pot and give it a swirl. A *gentle swirl*. Now, the sugar may look weird and crackly at this point, but don't worry. It'll all work out in the end. Soon, you'll notice that the bubbling sugar has turned into a bubbling foam, which means that you're getting very close. Watch for the color to turn to amber, and when it does, remove from the heat, add the butter and crème fraîche or sour cream, the sea salt, and stand back, so you don't get splattered. It'll bubble up like crazy, but don't worry. It'll also calm right down. Once it does, stir it up with your wooden spoon until the butter and crème fraîche or sour cream is completely incorporated. Pour this into a glass bowl to cool, and then refrigerate. To serve, simply rewarm the sauce over very low heat.

★ **COWGIRL TIP:** Use fleur de sel if you can for your Salty Caramel Sauce—it's clean and light and will make a huge difference.

FRENCH BISCOTTI

Cooked twice, so they're two times as crunchy as they'd otherwise be, biscotti are meant to be dipped right into your coffee—an espresso, a *noisette,* even a café au lait.

Not too sweet, with a hint of lemon and loaded with almonds, these French biscotti remind me of Tuscan *cantuccini,* but they have a finer crumb, they're flatter, and they're not nearly as hard.

My friend Catherine Chalverat brought these for us to share over coffee one morning after walking the dogs (hers is a black Lab named Ulysees) at Parc St. Cloud. "They're a special biscuit from Nîmes," she said. We dunked and crunched and kept on eating them long after the coffee was gone.

They're called *croquants villaret,* after the boulangerie that's been making them since 1775, before the French Revolution. A top secret recipe, the Web site said.

Not that secret. I found something that sounded similar, and went to work in the kitchen, adding this and taking away that.

Discovering regional specialties like these biscotti is one of the things I love most about France. Imagine: cookies made the same way for hundreds of years, from seventeenth-century wood-burning ovens to my Cowgirl kitchen in Paris and now to you. Generations of cookies and coffee and friendship. I just love that.

FRENCH BISCOTTI

MAKES ABOUT 5 DOZEN

1 stick/125 grams of butter

4 cups/500 grams of flour

$\frac{1}{4}$ teaspoon of sea salt

2 cups/200 grams of powdered sugar

2 eggs, lightly beaten

2 teaspoons of lemon juice

the zest of 1 lemon

$\frac{1}{4}$ cup/2 ounces/125 grams of unsalted whole almonds

1 egg white, whisked with a bit of water

1. Preheat the oven to 350°F/180°C, and line 2 cookie sheets with parchment paper (my favorite way).

2. Melt your butter over very low heat, then remove from heat and let cool.

3. Mix together the flour, sea salt, and powdered sugar. Pour in the eggs, the cooled butter, the lemon juice and zest and mix until combined and the dough changes from crumbly into a mass—this will take less than a minute. Add the almonds and smoosh them into the dough with your hands.

4. Divide the dough into 4 portions, and press each piece into a 3 x 12-inch/7.5 x 30.5 cm rectangle, about $\frac{1}{4}$-inch/6mm thick. I like to press this out and then use a small rolling pin to finish it off and make it smooth. You should be able to get 2 pieces of dough on each cookie sheet. Bake for 15 minutes, remove from the oven, and let cool for 2 minutes. Now, slice the dough into cookie fingers about $\frac{3}{4}$-inch/2 cm wide, and spread them a little on the cookie sheet so they have some breathing room. Brush the cookies with the egg white, and pop them back into the oven for about 20 to 25 minutes or until they're brown on the edges. Let them cool completely before you eat them—hopefully, with a cup of coffee for dunking. Store in an airtight jar.

WATERMELON GRANITA

Watermelons were Fourth of July food, a summer treat that was a production from beginning to end. Carried from the car to the house in an old red wagon. Too big for the fridge, they'd barely fit into our green metal Coleman cooler. You could never eat them the day they were bought. Cooling down a watermelon took a day, at least, back then.

Cold as ice, after being on ice, our watermelon was crisp, juicy, something to behold and to be eaten. We'd salt them if they were too sweet. I'd spit the slippery black seeds at my brother.

We ate them in big wedges on doubled-up paper plates that never did the job—they sagged, the pink juice spilling off the plate and onto the concrete, a sticky mess to clean up later. Not that I ever did.

Now watermelons aren't just pink, they're yellow, too. Skins of deep dark green, not just the two-tone stripes. I buy the smaller, refrigerator-size seedless for my watermelon granita, a fancy sounding thing, but just another way to ice down a melon. Chop it up, blend it, pour it into a box. Into the freezer instead of a Coleman cooler. Eaten with a spoon, out of a glass or a bowl, without so much as a drop on the ground. So civilized.

WATERMELON GRANITA

MAKES 6 TO 8 SERVINGS

½ of a small seedless watermelon
sea salt
about 8 fresh mint leaves, finely chopped,
  plus a bit more for serving
1¼ cups /300 grams of Greek yogurt
4 teaspoons of sugar (or more or less, to your taste)
½ teaspoon of vanilla extract

1. Cut your watermelon into big chunks (discard the rinds), and toss into
   the blender along with a pinch of salt and the mint. Purée until it's nice
   and smooth, pour it into a shallow plastic container, and slide this into
   the freezer. Every half-hour or so, take a fork and scrape the top. After 3
   to 4 hours, you'll have granita.

2. That was the hard part. Now, whisk together the yogurt, sugar, and
   vanilla. Simply layer the granita and the yogurt mixture in small see-
   through glasses, starting with a layer of the watermelon granita, and
   ending with the creamy yogurt. Top with a bit more chopped mint, and
   serve.

BROWN BUTTER WALNUT CAKES
(FINANCIERS AUX NOIX)

One Sunday afternoon, I talked X into going with me to a *marché des producteurs*, a market of food products sold by the actual producers: beekeepers with jars of honey and bars of soap made from beeswax; lavender growers from Provence with essential oils and dried lavender in cloth sacks; goose and pig farmers from the southwest with foie gras and artisanal sausages (which there always seem to be the most of).

When I saw a man selling walnuts and little walnut cakes from Périgord (where the best walnuts in France come from), I screeched to a stop, bought one, and ate it on the spot. Then I bought another.

Called a *financier aux noix*, this was a walnuty version of the classic French mini-loaf cake made with ground almonds called *financier*—so named because of its gold bar shape, and the long-held legend that these cakes were first made popular around Paris' financial district, near the stock exchange.

I bought two sacks of walnuts and started baking the next day. I roasted walnuts. I browned butter (there's a reason why this is called *beurre noisette* in French—it tastes just like hazelnuts). I got out my mini-muffin pans (I have not added financier pans to my ever-growing collection yet). The verdict? Nuttier, moister, and lighter. Round rather than rectangular didn't seem to make a bit of difference. If I sold these around La Bourse today, I might just start a whole new trend.

BROWN BUTTER WALNUT CAKES
(FINANCIERS AUX NOIX)
MAKES 2 DOZEN

2 sticks/250 grams of butter, plus more for buttering the muffin tin

5 ounces/140 grams of walnuts, toasted and finely ground

1 cup/200 grams of sugar

½ cup/70 grams of flour

½ teaspoon of sea salt

6 egg whites

1. Preheat the oven to 350°F/180°C and generously butter a 24-mini muffin tin.

2. To make the brown butter, melt your butter in a saucepan over low heat until it turns brown and begins to smell nutty—the butter should gurgle bubbles—this'll just take about 10 minutes. Whatever you do, don't try to rush this—or you'll end up with burned butter. Once it's brown and nutty, pour your butter into a bowl and let it cool.

3. In your mixer bowl, whisk together the walnuts, sugar, flour, and sea salt. Add the egg whites and mix well. Add the brown butter, and mix just until it comes together—don't overdo. Scoop the batter into your greased muffin tin, filling three-quarters to the top. Bake for 10 to 15 minutes, or until the edges start to brown and the little cakes' tummies rise up out of the pan—they really do this! Flip the pan over, whack it on your countertop, and the cakes should fall right out. Serve immediately—these are best the day that you make them.

FRENCH
CHOCOLATE SAUCE

In case of emergencies, something like this should be in the fridge at all times. To shake hot fudge sundae cravings. To pour over a cake or a tart. To eat by the spoonful at 4 in the afternoon, when you need something to go with that last coffee of the day.

My dad understood the need for chocolate sauce, and he made it often late at night. My brother and I would already be in our bedrooms doing homework, or pretending to, and then he'd call us down to the kitchen, and there they'd be, hot fudge sundaes for us all. The leftovers were kept in an old peanut butter jar in the fridge, which is how I learned about the value of chocolate sauce as an afternoon snack.

In France there are profiteroles, balls of puff pastry usually filled with vanilla ice cream and served with a polite drizzle of chocolate. Crêpes, too, come with chocolate sauce, and ice cream on the side if you ask for it. A shared love of chocolate may be the only thing my father had in common with the French.

There's nothing to making your own chocolate sauce. It takes minutes. But then you've got to decide: How much will you eat now and how much will you save for later?

FRENCH
CHOCOLATE SAUCE

MAKES ABOUT 1½ CUPS/360 ML

1 (7-ounce/200 gram) bar bittersweet
   chocolate (I use Lindt 70%)
½ cup/100 grams of sugar
¾ cup/180 ml of cream
3 tablespoons of butter
a small pinch of sea salt

Put all of the ingredients in a double boiler over medium-low heat (the
water shouldn't be boiling, but gently simmering), and stir until everything's melted and combined. Serve immediately over ice cream, or let cool
and refrigerate for later. To reheat, simply warm the sauce over low heat in
a double boiler.

★ **COWGIRL TIP:** This sauce is also great spread on your morning
toast, drizzled over oven-roasted pears, Grilled Orange-Vanilla Pound
Cake (p.280), or simply eaten by the spoonful, right out of the fridge.

BUTTERMILK ICE CREAM

I can still see my dad, opening our olive green side-by-side fridge, and pouring himself a tall glass of buttermilk, thick as a milkshake, and sprinkling it with salt. Mom would make a face because buttermilk was for cornbread and biscuits and for making cakes, not for drinking.

In Paris, buttermilk's tricky to find; it's called *lait fermenté*, or fermented milk, which is what it is, the leftover liquid from making butter, which is how the real stuff—not the manufactured stuff that we buy today—was made. I like the buttermilk best in the Arabic parts of town. It's sold right on the street in skinny green-and-white cartons during Ramadan, along with boxes of fresh dates still on the stems.

Like my mom, I'm not a buttermilk drinker; but like my dad, I love its subtle tang. Also like my dad, I eat a lot of ice cream, and I make a fresh batch just about every week. A carton of buttermilk in my fridge, some cream, and eggs are the start of cake batter for some; but these ingredients also happen to make some mighty fine ice cream, I learned. Tastes just like cake batter, in fact.

BUTTERMILK ICE CREAM

MAKES 1 QUART/1 LITER

2 cups /480 ml of cream
2 eggs
³/₄ cup/150 grams of sugar
a pinch of sea salt
1¹/₂ cups/360 ml of buttermilk

1. Warm your cream in a heavy saucepan over medium-low heat, and give it a stir every now and then so it doesn't scorch.

2. Beat the eggs in a bowl. Add the sugar and pinch of salt and mix this well.

3. When the cream begins to show tiny bubbles along the side, it's ready. You don't want this to boil.

4. Temper the eggs by slowly pouring a little cream into the bowl, and whisking quickly—if you've got someone to pour while you whisk, all the better. Then add the egg mixture back to saucepan and continue to cook for a few more minutes, just until the mixture begins to thicken.

5. Pour this through a strainer (to catch any pieces of cooked egg) into a bowl, then whisk in the buttermilk. Cool your mixture in an ice bath, then refrigerate for a couple of hours or until you're ready to make the ice cream. Freeze in your ice cream maker, and serve immediately for soft ice cream, or pop into the freezer for a few hours, then scoop.

MILKY WAY
ICE CREAM

Melanie was my best friend in fifth grade and still is today.

One summer, not long after we'd first struck up a friendship, she invited me to go with her family to her grandmother's house. She had just made ice cream—with Milky Way candy bars.

A few years ago, Melanie made dinner for X and me, and for dessert—and as a surprise—she made Milky Way ice cream. Decades later, it was even better than I remembered. Then I moved to Paris and she gave me the recipe. I started making it here with Milky Ways that I'd carry over in my suitcase or that friends would mule for me.

Before I served this for a dinner party one night, I worried that Milky Way ice cream was so entangled with my own fond memories that it might not be as good as I thought. But as one of our dinner guests went back to the kitchen for seconds and ended up licking the last remaining bits off of the dasher, I stopped worrying.

MILKY WAY ICE CREAM

MAKES 1 QUART/1 LITER

Adapted from Melanie Watson's grandmother's recipe.

4 (2.05-ounce) Milky Way bars
4 cups/1 liter of milk, divided
3 eggs
½ cup/100 grams of sugar
a pinch of sea salt
1 cup/240 ml of cream
1 teaspoon of vanilla extract

1. Slice your Milky Way bars into chunks and toss them into a small, heavy saucepan over low heat. Add 1 cup/240 ml of the milk and let this cook until the candy is melted, stirring every now and then.

2. In another heavy saucepan on low heat, scald the remaining 3 cups/720 ml of milk. (You'll know when the milk has scalded when you see tiny bubbles along the side.)

3. Beat the eggs in a bowl with the sugar and pinch of salt, and mix well.

4. Temper your eggs by pouring a little bit of the hot milk into the bowl, while continuing to whisk vigorously. Then add the eggs to the milk in the saucepan and cook for a few more minutes, until the custard begins to thicken. Remove the custard from the heat, pour it through a strainer set over a big bowl, and whisk in the cream and vanilla. Let this cool in an ice bath or simply on the countertop, then refrigerate for a few hours.

5. Once the Milky Way bars are melted, remove this mixture from the heat, too, let cool, and refrigerate until cold. (You keep the two mixtures separate until freezing.)

6. When you're ready to make your ice cream, pour the custard mixture into your ice cream freezer, and then pour in the melted Milky Way bars. It'll be ready soon. And you'll thank me for this one—and Melanie, and her sweet grandmother, Ma.

MASCARPONE MOUSSE *with* RASPBERRIES

Since X showed me the French way to eat chocolate mousse, spoonful by tiny spoonful, dunked in espresso, I've eaten more than a person should.

I ordered it wherever we went. I started making it at home. After a few years, though, I'd had enough. I'd had too much. I stopped eating chocolate mousse.

Then one summer, I saw a recipe in one of the French food magazines for a mousse made with mascarpone, the super-rich Italian cow's milk cheese that's really more like a crème fraîche. I'd not thought of mascarpone in years, not since my tiramisù phase.

Nothing to cook, just a few eggs to separate and whip into a frenzy. I made it once, twice, maybe three times in one month. That's not too much, is it?

MASCARPONE MOUSSE
WITH RASPBERRIES

MAKES 6 SERVINGS

3 room temperature eggs, separated
½ cup/100 grams of sugar
the zest of 1 lemon
8 ounces/225 grams of mascarpone cheese
sea salt
8 ounces/225 grams of fresh raspberries

1. Whisk together your egg yolks, sugar, lemon zest, and mascarpone until it's smooth.

2. In a very clean bowl, whip the egg whites with a pinch of salt, and when stiff peaks form, fold this into the mascarpone mixture. Cover with plastic wrap and refrigerate for at least 30 minutes. To serve, spoon the mousse into bowls, and add a small handful of raspberries to each one.

★ **COWGIRL TIP:** It's always best to use room temperature eggs for mousses, because they have more puff power.

CARAMEL
FLEUR DE SEL
POTS DE CRÈME

My grandmother Mary was a fiercely independent chocoholic, caffeine addict, and world traveler. No wonder I identified with her early on.

She was often gone for months at a time, traveling to Cairo, where she rode a camel in front of the pyramids; to Carnival in Rio de Janiero; and to Paris, where I still have a framed photograph of her standing in front of the Eiffel Tower on my wall.

When she wasn't packing or unpacking her bags, she gardened. She knitted. She was an avid reader. She rescued dogs, and cooked for them. She joined every woman's club that she could in Ardmore, Oklahoma, and led most of them. She drank strong black coffee from beans that she'd grind herself from morning till night. And she cooked for her family (she also burned a lot of what she made, tossing the blackened pans into the backyard, which my grandfather would retrieve and clean). Holidays were a formal affair, with more forks and spoons around each plate than I'd ever seen.

For dessert, she'd often make a chocolate meringue pie. But once, after a trip to France, she made chocolate pots de crème. She served them in mismatched porcelain demitasse cups, with the tiniest of spoons.

It was the richest, most elegant dessert I'd ever tasted. Nothing like Jello pudding from the box.

When I hosted my first cooking class in Paris, I wanted to make something special for dessert, and I remembered my grandmother Mary's pots de crème. But I made them with salty caramel instead of chocolate.

I'm pretty sure Mary would be fine with that.

CARAMEL FLEUR DE SEL POTS DE CRÈME

MAKES 6 SERVINGS

1¼ cups/250 grams of sugar
¼ cup/60 ml of water
1 teaspoon of fleur de sel, plus more for sprinkling on top
1½ cups/360 ml of cream
½ cup/120 ml of milk
6 egg yolks

1. Preheat your oven to 350°F/175°C.

2. Go ahead and put the sugar and water in a heavy deep pot, give it a stir, then turn the heat on medium-high, and leave it alone. It'll bubble continuously. Please don't stir the pot, as tempting as it may be. The less you mess with caramel, the better. After 10 to 15 minutes, the sugar will begin to darken, just around the sides, and I'll repeat: Don't stir. But, you may, if you want to (and usually I do), pick up the pot and give it a gentle swirl. Soon, you'll notice that the bubbling sugar has turned into a bubbling foam, which means that you're getting close. Watch for the color to turn to amber, and when it does, turn off the heat, add the cream and milk, and stand back. It'll bubble up like crazy, but don't worry. It'll also calm right down. Stir it with your wooden spoon until the cream and milk is completely incorporated. It'll just take a minute or two. Remove from the heat.

3. Beat the yolks in large bowl, then temper the eggs by adding just a tiny bit of the caramel mixture, so it comes to temperature and the eggs don't scramble. Slowly add the rest of the caramel to the eggs until incorporated.

4. Divide the mixture among 6 ½ cup/115 gram ramekins placed in a large roasting pan. Pour enough water into the pan to reach three-quarters up the sides of the ramekins, cover with foil, and slide into the oven. Bake just until custard is set at edges, but moves in center when shaken gently, about 45 minutes to 1 hour. Carefully remove the roasting pan from the oven. Take the custards out of the water, and let them cool on a towel on the counter. Once cooled to room temperature, cover each one with foil, and refrigerate for 2 hours, at least. Sprinkle each with a pinch of fleur de sel and serve with fresh strawberries, raspberries, and/or a spoonful of whipped cream.

★ **COWGIRL TIP:** No ramekins? No problem. Any heatproof ceramic or glass container will do.

PEACH CROUSTADE

I hate to admit to having favorites, but when it comes to summer fruit, peaches are at the top of my list. I eat them standing over the sink, juices dripping down my chin. I cut them up, and throw them in yogurt and smoothies. When I'm going to a little trouble, I make peach granitas or Peach-Tomato Chipotle Salsa (p.176).

When buying things like peaches, avocados, and mangoes I always buy the hardest ones, so I can put them in a big bowl on the kitchen table and babysit them as they become softer each day. But these French peaches are something else: They're hard as metal *boules* at the market, but once they're home, they quickly turn soft—within twenty-four hours. Texas peaches, they were different. Bigger, for one thing. Sweeter, and juicier, too. They were just happy to sit in my blue bowl and ripen at their own slow pace. These Paris peaches are in such a hurry.

Which is why I like to find the firmest ones that I can. At the markets here, that's a very big *non*.

After living here for five years, I know well that you're not supposed to touch the fruit and veggies at the market, but recently, at a stand that I'd frequented a few times already during peach season, I did the unthinkable. I reached across that invisible forbidden barrier between customer and vendor and *picked up a peach*. Of course, I didn't just walk up to the stand and grab a peach. That sort of behavior would certainly get me thrown out of the market and possibly right out of France. I was under the impression that this vendor and I had been building a relationship. On this particular day, I'd already complimented him on his wonderful cherries from the Loire and expressed great remorse that he didn't have any that week.

But he wasn't listening.

The Peach Man grabbed the peach from me, and scolded me harshly. *"Ne touche pas!"* he said, using the familiar *tu* form, since as we were already, as I mentioned, building a relationship, and were past the more formal *vous* standoffishness.

And for a moment, a brief nanosecond, I thought about walking away. I felt rejected. He didn't remember me.

But I knew his peaches were delicious. This was no time to make a stand or feel hurt. I told him that I'd take four, and I went home, put them in the bowl, and made this *croustade* the very next day.

A croustade is just like a pie or a tart, but flattened out and free-form, so you can bake it on a cookie sheet. It can be round or rectangular, small or large. Things don't get much simpler than this; it's just peaches and some buttery sweet dough, dusted with sugar so it crunches a little when you bite into it. It's not peach cobbler, but the idea is the same. Just peaches and dough, that's all. And if the peaches are good, that's enough.

PEACH CROUSTADE

MAKES 2; SERVES 4

1¼ cups/150 grams of flour

5 heaping tablespoons of sugar, plus a little more for sprinkling on the crust

a pinch of sea salt

1 stick/125 grams of butter, cut into small cubes and chilled

3 to 4 tablespoons of ice water

3 large peaches

a squeeze of lemon juice

1 egg white, whisked with a bit of water

powdered sugar

1. Whisk together your flour, 3 heaping tablespoons of sugar, and sea salt, or put this in a food processor and pulse a time or two. Add the butter

cubes and either with a pastry cutter or pulsing in a food processor, cut in the butter only until it looks like tiny pebbles throughout. Add the ice water by tablespoonfuls and mix just until the dough is still quite crumbly and you can pinch it together easily with your fingertips—you don't want it to be one big mass. Dump the dough bits directly onto a piece of plastic wrap and gently press it together into a nice fat disk. Wrap it up and pop into the fridge for an hour. (You can also do this a day in advance.)

2. Preheat your oven to 450°F/230°C and line a cookie sheet with parchment paper.

3. Just before you want to roll out your croustade, cut your peaches into thick slices and gently toss them with the lemon juice and remaining 2 tablespoons of sugar (you may need more depending on the sweetness of your peaches). You don't want to do this too far in advance, because the peaches will get too watery and you don't want watery peaches sogging up your crust.

4. You've got a choice. You can make 2 medium-size ones, or 4 smallish, individual ones—it's up to you. I usually go with 2 mediums. Whatever you decide, divide the dough accordingly, and put whatever you're not rolling out immediately back in the fridge. Now, on a lightly floured surface, roll out your dough into a roughly round shape—the beauty of making a croustade is that it's not meant to be perfect. Put the dough on the parchment-lined cookie sheet and heap as many peaches as will fit in the middle of the dough, leaving 2 inches/5 cm around the edges. Fold the edges of the dough over the peaches, brush the dough with the egg white mixture, and sprinkle a little bit of sugar on top. Slide into the oven for 25 to 30 minutes, or until the crust is brown. Serve warm, with a sprinkle of powdered sugar, and a scoop of ice cream.

> ★ **COWGIRL TIP:** Cut your butter into tiny cubes and pop into the freezer an hour before you make the dough, or even better—do this the day before.

CHAPTER 9

Tex-Mex 101

All of the recipes in this book are personal, but the ones in this chapter are even more so.

When I started making tortillas in my French cast-iron skillet made for crêpes, I reconnected with Texas. With its blazing sunshine and unforgiving summers, pitchers of margaritas and bowls of queso and salty tortilla chips still warm from the fryer. Those first tortillas forever changed how I saw Paris, and how I felt about being here. They made a very foreign-feeling place less so, and I suddenly felt less displaced and more at home, because I was making food from home. It wasn't long after that that I thought, if I could make tortillas, what else could I do?

So down the list I went. Salsas and guac, enchiladas, black beans, and chili. Making Tex-Mex in Paris wasn't as easy as making it back in Texas. Every ingredient had to be hunted down—black beans on one side of town, avocados and limes on another—but the scavenger hunt-style shopping became part of the fun. Even with all of the substitutions I had to make, these dishes weren't just stand-ins for what I remembered from home. They actually worked. So what if I was using Moroccan chiles when I needed jalapeños, and a mix of English cheddar and mozzarella instead of Monterey Jack? It was all good.

These recipes became the foundation of my first cooking classes here, which I called Tex-Mex 101.

They are the nuts and bolts of the Texas-based cuisine, loved by many, but still so misunderstood in France. I'm just happy to do my part helping to dispel the myths that guacamole comes in screw-top jars, and that fajitas are made from a kit that you buy at the Casino grocery store. It's no wonder that Parisians make a face every time I mention Tex-Mex. They don't know what it really is. Poor things.

WHEAT TORTILLAS

MAKES ABOUT 30 SMALL TORTILLAS

*I first learned to make flour tortillas many years ago
at Jane Butel's cooking class in Albuquerque, New Mexico, and I'll
never forget tasting that first homemade tortilla hot off the comal.
Here, I've taken Jane's recipe and tweaked it a bit to make it my own.
I like the flavor of wheat, but you can make these with all white flour
if you like, or add green chiles or chipotle chiles to the dough.*

2 cups/255 grams of whole wheat flour

2 cups/255 grams of flour

2 teaspoons of baking powder

1 teaspoon of salt

¼ cup /55 grams of lard, Crisco, or butter

1 to 1¼ cups /240 to 300 ml of warm water

1. Put your first 4 ingredients in a food processor and pulse a couple of
times to blend—or if you're doing this by hand, simply whisk it all
together. Add your lard, Crisco, or butter and mix it up only until the
mixture looks crumbly. Add the warm water slowly, and pay attention,
because you want the dough to come together and be only slightly sticky.

2. Let your dough have a siesta under a dish towel for about 15 minutes.

3. When you're ready to make the tortillas, tear off a ping-pong-ball-size
piece of dough, roll it into a ball, and put this back under the towel.
Repeat until you've made small balls out of the entire batch of dough.

4. Now, with your rolling pin, on a lightly floured surface, roll out each ball into a thin 6-inch/15 cm tortilla, and stack on a plate with parchment paper or wax paper between each one. I like to do all of my rolling out first; then I move on to cooking them all.

5. To cook the tortillas, heat up a cast-iron skillet or comal (or crêpe pan, if you're in France), and turn the heat to medium-high. Do not oil the pan. When the pan is nice and hot, put your circle of dough in the middle, wait for it to bubble, then flip. Stack your tortillas with pieces of parchment or wax paper in between each one, slide them into a plastic bag and store them in the fridge for a week, or in the freezer for a month or two. To reheat, simply place the tortillas on the hot cast-iron skillet, comal, or crêpe pan, or wrap in foil and pop into a 375°F/190°C oven for 10 to 15 minutes.

BACK IN BLACK BEANS

MAKES 6 TO 8 SERVINGS

I've come up with lots of recipes for black beans over the years, but this one, the most pared-down of them all, is what I like best, because this serves as a great base for so many other things—salsas, dips, refried beans, and anything else I can think of. More spices can always be added later.

olive oil
1 onion, chopped
2 cloves of garlic, minced
$\frac{1}{2}$ of a red bell pepper, diced
1 pound/500 grams of dried black beans
about 6 cups /1$\frac{1}{2}$ liters of water
sea salt and pepper

Drizzle a little olive oil in the bottom of a deep, large stockpot, add the onions and garlic, and turn the heat to medium. Cook for just a few minutes, until the onions become translucent. Add the red bell pepper, let this cook for a minute or two, then add your beans, water, and a big pinch of black pepper—not the salt yet, because I like to salt at the end. Let the beans come to a boil, reduce the heat to a simmer, cover (with the lid slightly askew), and let cook for 2 hours, or until your beans have that perfect "pop" of the skin when you bite into them, with soft insides.

CORN TORTILLAS

MAKES ABOUT 2 DOZEN SMALL TORTILLAS

$2\frac{1}{2}$ cups/625 grams of masa from white,
yellow, or blue corn

1 teaspoon of sea salt

$1\frac{1}{4}$ cups /300 ml of hot water

1. Cut 40 pieces of parchment or wax paper to put between your tortillas—
a 5 x 5 inch/12 x 12 cm square will work perfectly.

2. Mix up your masa and salt, then add the hot water a little at a time, until the
dough comes together. Test the dough by pinching off a piece and rolling it
into a ball, then flattening it with your palm. It shouldn't crack, but have
enough moisture to be pliable. If it's not, just mix in a little more water.

3. Tear off a golf ball-size piece of dough, and roll it into a ball. Keep the rest
of the dough covered with a damp kitchen towel so it doesn't dry out.
Using a tortilla press, put 1 piece of parchment on the bottom, add the
ball of dough, and put a second sheet of parchment or wax paper on top.
Press down the tortilla press and when it feels like it's as far down as it
can go, give it a little shimmy and move it from side to side—this will
help flatten the tortillas a bit more. Remove the tortilla with the parchment attached, and repeat with the rest of the dough.

4. Using an ungreased comal or cast-iron skillet, over medium-high heat,
cook your tortillas for a minute or two on the first side, or until you see
the edges just begin to lift up—this is very subtle, but it's a great clue to
the tortillas' readiness. You don't want these to get brown, but merely to
cook through. Flip them over, let them cook for about 20 more seconds,
then stack them on a plate, with parchment in between each one. Store
your tortillas in a plastic bag in the fridge for a couple of weeks or in the
freezer for up to 6 months.

TAQUERIA SALSA

MAKES ABOUT 4 CUPS/1 QUART/1 LITER

This salsa is made from pickled jalapeños, which I realize sounds weird, but that's all I've got in Paris. By all means, if you've got fresh, use them here.

1 tablespoon of vegetable oil
1 onion, roughly chopped
2 cloves of garlic, minced
1 (28-ounce/765 gram) can of diced tomatoes
2 pickled jalapeños
a big handful of fresh cilantro
sea salt and pepper

Put the vegetable oil in a saucepan and add your onions and garlic. Turn the heat to medium-low, and cook for a few minutes, just until the onions become translucent. Add your tomatoes, jalapeños, cilantro, a big pinch of salt and an even bigger pinch of pepper. Let this cook for about 5 minutes, then purée with a hand blender. Serve warm for maximum fun. Put any left-over salsa in an old jam jar in the fridge; it'll keep for a few days just fine.

★ **SWAP IT:** No jalapeños? Use serranos or chipotles instead.

ROASTED
SALSA VERDE

MAKES ABOUT 2 CUPS/480 ML

*Sadly, Paris is just as tomatillo-poor as it is jalapeño-deprived,
so I make this when I'm back in Texas, and put it on everything I can
think of, from scrambled eggs to leftover chicken, shoved in a tortilla.*

**1 pound/500 grams of tomatillos,
husks removed and rinsed**

2 cloves of garlic, unpeeled

½ of an onion, sliced in a few big pieces

2 fresh jalapeños

a handful of fresh cilantro

sea salt

1. Roast your tomatillos, garlic, onion, and jalapeños on an ungreased comal or cast-iron skillet, over medium-high heat. This'll only take about 15 minutes, and you may need to do this in batches—the tomatillos first, and then the rest.

2. Peel the garlic and put everything but the jalapeños in a medium bowl.

3. Cut off the stems of the jalapeños, slice them open, and take out the seeds and membranes if you want a milder salsa; don't mess with them if you like it hot. Toss your peppers in with the onions and garlic.

4. Add a big handful of cilantro to the bowl, and with a hand blender, mix everything together—but not too much, because you'll want this to be chunky—and season with a pinch of salt. I love this salsa with everything, and like it especially warmed up—with chips, over eggs, on tacos, you name it. Keep this in the fridge and if you want to warm it up the next day, you'll need to add just a little bit of water; it thickens up like crazy.

HOLY GUACAMOLE!

MAKES 4 SERVINGS

*There are lots of variations on guacamole, and many include
onions and jalapeños, but I like mine without, simply because
usually when I'm eating guac, I'm also eating spicy salsas and pico,
so I like the guac to be something that's cool on the plate.*

4 ripe avocados

1 tomato, diced

2 cloves of garlic, minced

a small handful of cilantro, chopped

the juice of 1 lime

sea salt and pepper

1. Cut your avocados in half and scoop out the flesh into a bowl. With two
knives, simply cut and slice until the avocados are in small pieces—but
not too much, because we want this to be chunky.

2. Gently fold in the rest of the ingredients. Taste. Refrigerate for an hour
before serving.

> ★ **COWGIRL TIP**: Don't worry about saving the pit to keep the guac
> from turning brown—invest in some good plastic wrap instead. Smash
> the wrap down onto the surface of the guac so there's no air between the
> plastic and the guac; then put another piece on top of the bowl. It'll keep
> for a couple of days.

PICO DE GALLO

MAKES 4 SERVINGS

This is one of those recipes that you'll "see" when it's ready.
The ratio of tomatoes to onions is a little less than two to one,
(and of course, it depends on the size of your tomatoes and the onions)
but just remember the red of the tomatoes is the dominant color, and
there should be flecks of white onion and green cilantro throughout.

3 tomatoes, diced
1 onion, diced
1 clove of garlic, minced
1 to 2 jalapeños, finely chopped
a small handful of fresh cilantro, chopped
the juice of 1 to 2 limes
sea salt

Throw your tomatoes, onion, garlic, jalapeños, and cilantro into a bowl.
Add the lime juice and a big pinch of sea salt, and give it a taste. Add more
lime if you need to, or if you like more cilantro, toss it in, too. Refrigerate
for an hour before serving.

TEXAS CHILI

MAKES ABOUT 4 QUARTS/4 LITERS

*I've been making this chili for years, and usually with turkey,
because it's just a slightly lighter, healthier spin on the Texas classic,
plus you've already read my rant on French beef (p. 266). Feel free to add
jalapeños or chipotles if you want something spicier, but I like to create a
bowl that's not too hot, so folks can turn up the heat if they want.*

2 tablespoons of vegetable oil

1 onion, diced

4 to 5 cloves of garlic, minced

2 pounds/1 kilo of ground chuck mixed
   with ground sirloin (or use ground
   turkey, which I often use in France)

½ of a green bell pepper, diced

¼ of a red bell pepper, diced

3 (14.5-ounce/395 gram) cans kidney beans,
   black beans, or a mixture of the two, drained,
   then rinsed

2 (28-ounce/765 gram) cans of diced tomatoes

1 (6-ounce/170 gram) can of tomato paste

5 tablespoons of chili powder

1 teaspoon of cayenne pepper

2 teaspoons of cumin

2 teaspoons of dried oregano

1 teaspoon of smoky Spanish paprika or
   ancho chile powder

2 teaspoons of sea salt

2 cups/480 ml of water

1. Put the vegetable oil in a heavy, deep stockpot and add your onions and garlic. Turn the heat to medium-low and cook until the onions become translucent, just a few minutes. Stir in the ground beef (or the ground turkey) and cook until browned if you're using beef. (Or if you're using turkey, until it's cooked through and no longer pink.)

2. Toss in your red and green bell peppers, beans, tomatoes, tomato paste, spices, salt, and water. Turn the heat down to low and cook for a couple of hours, adjusting seasonings if you need to along the way.

★ **DOUBLE-DUTY:**

1. For chili-cheese soft tacos, spoon your chili onto a flour tortilla, add shredded lettuce, chopped tomatoes, avocado, and cheddar cheese. Serve with your favorite salsa.

2. Toss some tortilla chips on a heatproof plate. Spoon the chili on top, along with some grated cheese and jalapeño slices. Slide under the broiler until it melts.

3. Make single-serving Frito pies. Layer Fritos in the bottom of a ramekin, add chili and shredded cheese, and repeat. Bake at 375°F/190°C until bubbly. Serve with chopped green onion.

4. Make cheesy-chili macaroni, by adding chili to your favorite mac 'n cheese recipe.

5. Add chili to a hot dog or a burger—messy, but good.

6. Stir some chili into your queso.

7. Add a couple of poached eggs to your chili.

COWGIRL CHORIZO

2 POUNDS/ 1 KILO

After living in Paris a couple of years, I realized there would never
be a Spanish chorizo that equaled the Mexican chorizo I craved, so I
decided to make my own. This is spicy, but not spicy-hot, allowing the
smokiness of the paprika and the subtle hint of cinnamon to peek through.

2 pounds/1 kilo of ground pork

2 tablespoons of chili powder

2 tablespoons of smoky Spanish paprika
or ancho chile powder

1 teaspoon of dried oregano

1 teaspoon of garlic powder

½ teaspoon of ground cinnamon

2 tablespoons of red wine vinegar

2 teaspoons of sea salt

1. Smoosh everything together in a big bowl with your hands—there's no other way to do this.

2. Make a small chorizo patty and cook it up in a skillet and taste for seasonings. Now, you have a choice. You can either: 1) cook up your chorizo and pop into the freezer for 1 to 2 months, which is what I do, or 2) simply freeze the uncooked chorizo for 1 to 2 months, then thaw and cook when ready to use.

ADOBO SALSA

MAKES ABOUT 2 CUPS/480 ML

I learned to make this sauce at Culinario Centro Ambrosia in Mexico City, and it's great for marinating meats and spooning over enchiladas or tacos.

5 dried guajillo chiles
3 dried ancho chiles
2 dried cascabel chiles
2 cups/480 ml of boiling water
3 cloves of garlic, peeled
1 teaspoon of cumin seed
1 teaspoon of peppercorns
1 teaspoon of dried oregano
1 tablespoon of apple cider vinegar
sea salt

1. With your kitchen scissors, split open your dried chiles, throw away the stems and remove the seeds and veins. Give the chiles a quick rinse.

2. Get out your comal or cast-iron skillet, and turn the heat to medium-low. Once the surface is hot, put your split-open chiles directly onto the hot, ungreased surface, and use a wooden spoon to press them back down when they curl up from the heat. They're ready to flip to the other side when they begin to change color. This won't take long—around 30 seconds per side. Watch closely, and make sure your skillet doesn't get too hot, because the chiles will burn easily. Once the chiles are toasted, put them in a bowl and cover with the boiling water. Let them rest for 15 minutes.

3. Toast the garlic on the comal, then your cumin seeds and peppercorns. Put all of this in your blender.

4. Add your softened chiles and a little bit of the chile water to the blender, along with the oregano, and apple cider vinegar, and turn it on high. Add a big pinch of sea salt and more chile water, if needed, to blend easily. Keep the blender going until the mixture is super-smooth—give it at least 5 minutes. Have patience. The longer this blends, the more complex the flavors will be.

★ **ADVANCE PLANNING:** This sauce will freeze for about 6 months, or keep in the fridge for a couple of weeks.

Epilogue

Life's a lot like cooking, I've learned.

Take chocolate cake. Even with a trusted recipe, the right ingredients, a perfect pan, and a reliable oven, you never know how it'll turn out. Will it be the gâteau of your dreams? Or will it sink below your worst fears?

I followed my heart to France with my heart set on romantic, barefoot strolls along the sandy beaches of Normandy…and found myself instead in my cowboy boots in a cramped kitchen in Paris.

Turns out, moving to France was the best bad decision I ever made. Can't wait to see what I'll cook up next…

Acknowledgments

Big hugs to the team at Running Press: Jennifer Kasius, my wonderful editor; Amanda Richmond, my book designer, who understood my funky part cowgirl, part French flea market aesthetic; and photographer Steve Legato, whose beautiful food photographs are surpassed only by his superb air guitar playing.

Thank you to my fantastic agent, Doe Coover, who loved the Cowgirl Chef cookbook idea from the start.

A big merci to my food pals in Paris and France who offered support along the way: Dorie Greenspan, who was always available for coffee and encouragement; David Lebovitz, Clotilde Desoulier, Alisa Morov, Julie Mautner, and Kate Hill. And to my friends on both sides of the pond who cheered me on: Catherine Chalverat, Suzanne Allen, Julie Nauman, Melinda Meador, Debbie Gabriel, Gregory Edmont, Karen Eubank, Stephanie Chambers, Rebecca Sherman, Andrea Beane, Marissa Wallace, and Michael Tucker.

To X, my chief dish washer.

Thank you to my recipe testers Melanie Watson, David Acree, and Stephanie Doublait.

And to my Texas-based web support team, all of whom kept the Cowgirl Chef website running smoothly: Lisa Lawless, Dan Langendorf, and Wes Phelan.

Margaret Brown encouraged me to write this book in the first place. Thank you, Margaret.

To my friend and editor Dana Joseph, who told me years ago that I should write about food, because she saw this was my passion. Dana helped shape this book into what it is today; she gave her eyes and heart to this project as if it were her own.

Lastly, to my family: To my late father, who gave me a cookbook each year for Christmas as long as I can remember; and to my mom, who always encouraged me to play…in the kitchen and elsewhere.

I thank you all.

Index

A

Adobo Salmon Salad Tartines, **192**, 193–194

Adobo Salsa, 323–324

Appetizers, 23–55
  Basil Pesto Matchsticks, 38, 39–40
  Cheesy Rosemary-Olive Flatbread, 48, 49–51
  Chicken Empanadas with Cilantro Yogurt, 44, 45–47
  Eggplant Caviar, 36–37
  Mushroom Tapenade, 42–43
  Sweet Pea Pesto, 32–33
  Sweet Potato Biscuits with Ham, 28–30
  Texas Killers, 26–27
  Tiny Tarts, 53–55
  Toasted Pita Chips, 34–35

Apple Cider Vinaigrette, 147

Arugula Pesto, 196

Asian Chicken Salad with Ginger-Lime Vinaigrette, 148–149

Asparagus & Avocado Salad, 133–134

B

Back in Black Beans, 314

Basics, cooking, 14–16

Basil Oil, 97

Basil Pesto, 41

Basil Pesto Matchsticks, 38, 39–40

Basil Pesto Vinaigrette, 129

Basque-Style Fish En Papilotte, 270, 271–272

Beans, Back In Black, 314

Beef
  Bistro-Style Steak, 243
  Corona Beer-Braised Brisket Tacos, 154–156
  Steak Frîtes with Roquefort Sauce, 242–244
  Texas Chili, 320–321
  Tex-Mex Meatloaf, 266–267

Beets & Clementine Salad, **130**, 131–132

Beginnings, 6–13

Biscotti, French, 288–289

Bistro-Style Steak, 243

Black-Eyed Peas and Jalapeño Cornbread, 208–210

Black-Eyed Peas, Mom's, 209

BLT Tartines, Winter, 195–196

Breads
  Cheesy Rosemary-Olive Flatbread, 48, 49–51
  Cornbread Madeleines, **62**, 63–64
  Jalapeño Cornbread, 208, 210
  Sweet Potato Biscuits with Ham, 28–30

Brie and Prosciutto Sandwiches, Grilled, 189–190

Broccoli-Basil Soup with Goats Cheese Toasts, 95–96

Broccoli-Red Bell Pepper Tart, **180**, 181–183

Brussels Sprouts with Hazelnuts, 227–229

Buckwheat Crêpes with Ham, Guyère and Egg, 261–263

Buttermilk Ice Cream, 297–298

Butternut Squash, Spinach and Bacon

Salad, 144, 145–146

C

Cakes. *See also* Desserts
  Brown Butter Walnut Cakes, **292**,
    293–294
  Grilled Orange-Vanilla Pound Cake
    with Strawberries, 279–281
  Half-Baked Chocolate Cakes, 282–283
Caramel Fleur De Sel Pots De Crème,
  303–305
Caramel Sauce, 287
Cauliflower Galettes with Chipotle
  Crème Fraîche, **202**, 203–205
Cheese Tartines, Jalapeño Pimento,
  186–188
Cheesy Rosemary-Olive Flatbread, 48,
  49–51
Cherry Compote, 277–278
Chicken
  Asian Chicken Salad with Ginger-
    Lime Vinaigrette, 148–149
  Chicken Empanadas with Cilantro
    Yogurt, **44**, 45–47
  Fried Chicken Bites with Cream
  Gravy, 258–260
  Minestrone, 101–103
  Paris Chicken Fricassée, **72**, 73–74
  Perfect Roast Chicken, 264–265
  Skin and Bones Chicken Stock,
    111–112
  Smokin' Tortilla Soup, **86**, 87–88
  Tex-Mex Tart, 175–176
  Zucchini-Cilantro Soup, **104**, 105–
    107
Chili, Texas, 320–321
Chipotle Crème Fraîche, 205
Chipotle Salsa, 176
Chocolate Cakes, Half-Baked, 282–283
Chorizo, Cowgirl, 322
Cilantro Yogurt, 47

Cookies
  Slice and Bake Hazelnut-Chocolate
    Chip Cookies, 65–67
  Texas Killers, 26–27
Cooking tips, 18–21
Cooking utensils, 14–16
Cornbread, Jalapeño, 208, 210
Cornbread Madeleines, **62**, 63–64
Corona Beer-Braised Brisket Tacos,
  154–156
Cowgirl Chimichurri, 253
Cowgirl Chorizo, 322
Cowgirl Quiche, 59–60, **61**
Crêpes with Ham, Guyère and Egg,
  261–263

D

Deep South Salad, 150–151
Desserts, 275–309
  Brown Butter Walnut Cakes, **292**,
    293–294
  Buttermilk Ice Cream, 297–298
  Caramel Fleur De Sel Pots De Crème,
    303–305
  Cherry Compote, 277–278
  French Biscotti, 288–289
  French Chocolate Sauce, 295–296
  Grilled Orange-Vanilla Pound Cake
    with Strawberries, 279–281
  Half-Baked Chocolate Cakes, 282–283
  Mascarpone Mousse with Raspberries,
    301–302
  Milky Way Ice Cream, 299–300
  Peach Croustade, **306**, 307–309
  Peanut Butter-Chocolate Soufflés,
    69–70
  Rice Pudding with Salty Caramel
    Sauce, **284**, 285–287
  Watermelon Granita, 290–291
Dressings and Vinaigrettes
  Apple Cider Vinaigrette, 147
  Basil Oil, 97

Basil Pesto Vinaigrette, 129
Champagne-Honey Vinaigrette, 81
EZ French Vinaigrette, 126
Ginger-Lime Vinaigrette, 149
Hazelnut Vinaigrette, 229
Jalapeño-Cilantro Buttermilk
    Dressing, 140
Lime-Cilantro Oil, 135
Orange Vinaigrette, 123

E
Eggplant Caviar, 36–37

F
Fish and Seafood
    Adobo Salmon Salad Tartines, **192,**
        193–194
    Basque-Style Fish En Papilotte, **270,**
        271–272
    Fish Tacos with Mango-Avocado
        Salsa, **168,** 169–170
    Provencal Fish Stew, 248–250
    Salmon with Kalamata Olive-Basil
        Salsa, 268–269
    Salmon with Lentils, 245–247
    Sunday Tuna Salad, 119–121
French Biscotti, 288–289
French Chocolate Sauce, 295–296
French Lentils, 247
French Salad, My Big Fat, **78,** 79–81

G
Gazpacho, 93–94
Green Beans, French Bistro, 218–219
Greens and Salads, 117–151
    Asian Chicken Salad with Ginger-
        Lime Vinaigrette, 148–149
    Asparagus & Avocado Salad, 133–134
    Basil Pesto Vinaigrette, 129
    Beets & Clementine Salad, 131–132

Deep South Salad, 150–151
End of Summer Salad, 128–129
End of Winter Salad, 141–142
EZ French Vinaigrette, 126
It's the Berries Salad, **122,** 122–123
Le Halles Spinach Salad, 124–125
Lime-Cilantro Oil, 135
Orange Vinaigrette, 123
Purple Roquefort Slaw, 163–164
Roasted Butternut Squash, Spinach
    and Bacon Salad, **144,** 145–146
Sunday Tuna Salad, 119–121
Texas Pickup Salad, **138,** 139–140
Throw-Together Salad, 136–137

H
Hazelnut-Chocolate Chip Cookies,
    65–67

I
Ice Cream, Buttermilk, 297–298
Ice Cream, Milky Way, 299–300
It's the Berries Salad, **122,** 122–123

J
Jalapeño Pimento Cheese Tartines,
    186–188
Jalapeño-Cilantro Buttermilk Dressing,
    140

K
Kitchen basics, 14–16
Kitchen tips, 18–21

L

Lamb, Toni's, **238**, 239–241
Lamb Chops with Cowgirl Chimichurri, 251–253
Le Halles Spinach Salad, 124–125
Lime-Cilantro Oil, 135

M

Mascarpone Mousse with Raspberries, 301–302
Minestrone, 101–103
Minty Cantaloupe Soup, **98**, 99–100
Mushroom Tapenade, 42–43

O

Okra and Tomatoes, Roasted, 212–213

P

Paris Chicken Fricassée, **72**, 73–74
Peach Croustade, **306**, 307–309
Peanut Butter-Chocolate Soufflés, 69–70
Pecans, Happy Dance, 92
Pita Chips, Toasted, 34–35
Polenta Tart Crust, 183
Pork
    Buckwheat Crêpes with Ham, Guyère and Egg, 261–263
    Cowgirl Chorizo, 322
    Gascon-Style Pork Chops with Pepper Honey, **254**, 255–257
    Grilled Brie, Pear and Prosciutto Sandwiches, 189–190
    Sweet Potato Biscuits with Ham, 28–30
    Tacos Al Pastor, 157–159
    Tex-Mex Meatloaf, 266–267
    Winter BLT Tartines, 195–196
Potatoes, Green Chile-Goat Cheese Smashed, 216–217
Potatoes, Oven-Roasted Pommes Frîtes, 244
Potatoes, Rosemary, 224–225
Pound Cake with Strawberries, 279–281
Prosciutto and Brie Sandwiches, Grilled, 189–190
Provencal Fish Stew, 248–250

Q

Quiche, Cowgirl, 59–60, **61**

R

Ratatouille, Roasted, 230–231
Rice Pudding with Salty Caramel Sauce, **284**, 285–287
Roast Chicken, 264–265
Roasted Broccoli-Red Bell Pepper Tart, 180
Roasted Red Bell Pepper Mayo, 188
Roquefort Sauce, 243–244
Roquefort Slaw, Purple, 163–164

S

Salads, 117–151
    Asian Chicken Salad with Ginger-Lime Vinaigrette, 148–149
    Asparagus & Avocado Salad, 133–134
    Beets & Clementine Salad, **130**, 131–132
    Crunchy Grated Carrot Salad with Lime, 76–77
    Deep South Salad, 150–151
    End of Summer Salad, 128–129
    End of Winter Salad, 141–142
    It's the Berries Salad, **122**, 122–123
    Le Halles Spinach Salad, 124–125
    My Big Fat French Salad, **78**, 79–81
    Purple Roquefort Slaw, 163–164

Roasted Butternut Squash, Spinach and Bacon Salad, **144**, 145–146
Salmon Salad Tartines, **192**, 193–194
Sunday Tuna Salad, 119–121
Texas Pickup Salad, **138**, 139–140
Throw-Together Salad, 136–137
Salmon Salad Tartines, 193–194
Salmon with Kalamata Olive-Basil Salsa, 268–269
Salmon with Lentils, 245–247
Salty Caramel Sauce, 287
Sauces and Salsa
   Adobo Salsa, 323–324
   Arugula Pesto, 196
   Basil Pesto, 41
   Cilantro Yogurt, 47
   Cowgirl Chimichurri, 253
   French Chocolate Sauce, 295–296
   Holy Guacamole!, 318
   Mango-Avocado Salsa, **168**, 169–170
   Olive-Basil Salsa, 268–269
   Peach-Tomato Chipotle Salsa, 176
   Pepper Honey, 257
   Pico De Gallo, 319
   Roasted Red Bell Pepper Mayo, 188
   Roasted Salsa Verde, 317
   Roquefort Sauce, 243–244
   Salty Caramel Sauce, 287
   Taqueria Salsa, 316
Seafood. *See* Fish and Seafood
Skin and Bones Chicken Stock, 111–112
Soups, 83–115
   30-Minute Tomato Soup with Grilled Cheese Croutons, 108–110
   Broccoli-Basil Soup with Goats Cheese Toasts, 95–96
   Gazpacho, 93–94
   Minestrone, 101–103
   Minty Cantaloupe Soup, 98
   Skin and Bones Chicken Stock, 111–112
   Smokin' Tortilla Soup, **86**, 87–88
   Sweet Potato-Buttermilk Soup, 90–91
   Veggie Stock, 113–114

Zucchini-Cilantro Soup, **104**
Spinach, Potato and Caramelized Onion Tacos, 165–167
Spinach and Roquefort Tart, 177–178
Squash Soufflé, 232–233
Steak Frîtes with Roquefort Sauce, 242–244
Super-Quick Homemade Ricotta, 173
Sweet Pea Pesto, 32–33
Sweet Potato Biscuits with Ham, 28–30
Sweet Potato-Buttermilk Soup, 90–91
Sweet Potatoes with Cocoa Nibs, 214–215

T
Tacos
   Corona Beer-Braised Brisket Tacos, 154–156
   Fish Tacos with Mango-Avocado Salsa, **168**, 169–170
   Spinach, Potato and Caramelized Onion Tacos, 165–167
   Tacos Al Pastor, 157–159
   Tacos Carnitas with Purple Roquefort Slaw, **160**, 161–164
Tarts and Tartines
   Adobo Salmon Salad Tartines, 193–194
   Jalapeño Pimento Cheese Tartines, 186–188
   Polenta Tart Crust, 183
   Roasted Broccoli-Red Bell Pepper Tart, **180**, 181–183
   Roasted Red Bell Pepper Mayo, 188
   Roasted Veggie Melt, 184–185
   Spinach and Roquefort Tart, 177–178
   Tex-Mex Tart, 175–176
   Tiny Tarts, 53–55
   Tomato-Ricotta Tart, 171–173
   Whole Wheat-Oatmeal Tart Crust, 179
   Winter BLT Tartines, 195–196
Texas Chili, 320–321

Texas Killers, 26–27
Texas Pickup Salad, **138**, 139–140
Tex-Mex Dishes, 311–325
    Adobo Salsa, 323–324
    Back In Black Beans, 314
    Corn Tortillas, 315
    Cowgirl Chorizo, 322
    Holy Guacamole!, 318
    Pico De Gallo, 319
    Roasted Salsa Verde, 317
    Taqueria Salsa, 316
    Texas Chili, 320–321
    Tex-Mex Meatloaf, 266–267
    Tex-Mex Tart, 175–176
    Wheat Tortillas, 312–313
Tomato Gratin, 206–207
Tomato Soup with Grilled Cheese
    Croutons, 108–110
Tomatoes and Okra, Roasted, 212–213
Tomato-Ricotta Tart, 171–173
Tortilla Soup, Smokin', **86**
Tortilla Strips, Toasty, 89
Tortillas, Corn, 315
Tortillas, Wheat, 312–313
Trail guide, 18–21
Tuna Salad, Sunday, 119–121

V
Vegetable Side Dishes, 199–233
    Black-Eyed Peas and Jalapeño Corn-
    bread, 208–210
    Cauliflower Galettes with Chipotle
    Crème Fraîche, **202**, 203–205
    Cherry Tomato Gratin, 206–207
    Chipotle Crème Fraîche, 205
    French Bistro Green Beans, 218–219
    Green Chile-Goat Cheese Smashed
    Potatoes, 216–217
    Jalapeño Cornbread, 210
    Maple-Whipped Sweet Potatoes with
    Cocoa Nibs, 214–215
    My Grandmother's Yellow Squash
    Soufflé, 232–233
    Pan-Roasted Brussels Sprouts with
    Hazelnuts, 227–229
    Roasted Okra and Tomatoes, 212–213
    Roasted Ratatouille, 230–231
    Rosemary Potatoes, 224–225
    Stuffed Zucchini, **220**, 221–223
Veggie Melt, Roasted, 184–185
Veggie Stock, 113–114

W
Walnut Cakes, Brown Butter, **292**, 293–
    294
Watermelon Granita, 290–291

Z
Zucchini, Stuffed, **220**, 221–223
Zucchini-Cilantro Soup, **104**, 105–107

NOTES

NOTES

NOTES